Also by
The Beardstown Ladies' Investment Club

The Beardstown Ladies'
Common-Sense Investment Guide

The Beardstown Ladies'
Guide to Smart Spending for Big Savings

The
Beardstown Ladies'
Stitch-in-Time
Guide to Growing
Your Nest Egg

The Beardstown Ladies'

STITCH-IN-TIME GUIDE TO GROWING YOUR NEST EGG

xxxxxxxxxxxxxxxx

Step-by-Step Planning for a Comfortable Financial Future

xxxxxxxxxxxxxxxx

The Beardstown Ladies' Investment Club
with Robin Dellabough

A SETH GODIN PRODUCTION

NEW YORK

Table 2-1 and Figures 2.1 and 2.2 reprinted with permission from Franklin Templeton Distributors, Inc.

Figure 6.2 reprinted with permission from A. G. Edwards.

Excerpt from *Where to Retire* on page 164 reprinted by permission.

Excerpt from The Retirement Letter on page 164 reprinted by permission.

Illustrations by Mary A. Wirth
Design by Beth Tondreau Design/Mary A. Wirth

LIBRARY OF CONGRESS CATALOGING-IN-PUBLICATION DATA

Dellabough, Robin
    The Beardstown ladies' stitch-in-time guide to growing your nest egg : step-by-step planning for a comfortable financial future / The Beardstown Ladies' Investment Club with Robin Dellabough.
        p.   cm.
    "A Seth Godin Production."
    Includes bibliographical references and index.
    ISBN 0-7868-6192-4
    1. Investments—Handbooks, manuals, etc.   2. Finance, Personal—Handbooks, manuals, etc.   I. Beardstown Ladies Investment Club.
    II. Title.
    HG4527.D45   1996
    332.024'01—dc20   95–40451
                                                          CIP

Paperback ISBN: 0-7868-8186-0
10 9 8 7 6 5 4 3 2 1

We dedicate this book to Lillian Ellis, a charter member and past senior partner of the Beardstown Business and Professional Women's Investment Club, whose sudden death on October 19, 1994, left a void in our club and in our hearts. Lillian found great joy in her retirement. She managed her own investments with much success, followed the market, and willingly shared her knowledge. She would have loved contributing to the contents of this book.

—The Beardstown Ladies

ACKNOWLEDGMENTS

_____

From the Beardstown Ladies:

Homer G. Rieken, Broker, A.G. Edwards & Sons, Inc.
Homer helped us organize our investment club, encouraged us
to join the National Association of Investors Corporation, and has
been a trusted friend and supporter.

Havana National Bank, Havana, Illinois
Its wonderful reception and support of Betty enabled her to
share her knowledge throughout the book and at many
promotional events and education programs.

Beardstown Chamber of Commerce, Beardstown, Illinois
Donna Strieker, Secretary
Donna has worked many, many hours answering the enormous
amount of fan mail and telephone calls. She has mailed videos
and books around the world.

First Evangelical Lutheran Church, Beardstown, Illinois,
provided a monthly meeting room.

CIPS Company, Western Division, Beardstown, Illinois,
provided a room for our expanded "guest nights."

From the writer:

At Hyperion: Bob Miller and Laurie Abkemeier, Lisa Kitei, Simone Cooper and Kris Kliemann, for their good work and enthusiasm.

Leslie W. Lindeman and Meryl Davids, for invaluable editorial and research assistance.

Financial planners W. Lee Richardson, Frank Sisco, and Steven Klimaszewski, for their expertise, insight, and number crunching.

Jon Berry, for his generosity, patience, and ability to listen.

At Central Picture:
Keith Colter and Carolyn Patterson, for their continuing interest in and support of The Beardstown Ladies.

At Seth Godin Productions:
Seth Godin, Lisa DiMona, Audrey Delphendahl, Julie Maner, Karen Watts, Nicole Goldstein, Cynthia Liu, Shelby Watts, for their help and support, both general and specific, above and beyond . . .

And most of all, Eugene and Norma Berry, for being the best of all possible in-laws.

CONTENTS

_ _ _ _ _ _ _ _ _ _ _ _ _ _ _ _

THE BEARDSTOWN LADIES' INVESTMENT CLUB   XI

INTRODUCTION:
Beardstown and Beyond   1

CHAPTER ONE
Make Hay While the Sun Shines:
Financial Planning Means Many Different Things   10

CHAPTER TWO
A Penny Saved Is a Penny Earned:
Take Advantage of Compound Interest   26

CHAPTER THREE
Leave No Stone Unturned:
You May Have More Than You Think   44

CHAPTER FOUR
Cut the Cloth According to the Cloth:
Pay Yourself First   62

CHAPTER FIVE
Put the Horse Before the Cart:
Avoid Tax on Your Investment   76

CHAPTER SIX

Don't Put All Your Eggs in One Basket:

Diversify Your Investments to Limit Risk   90

CHAPTER SEVEN

The Long and the Short of It:

There's Somewhere for Everyone to Invest   104

CHAPTER EIGHT

Home is Where the Heart Is:

The Great Savings Engine   120

CHAPTER NINE

You Can't Take It With You:

Remember the Reason for Estate Planning,

Wills, and Insurance   136

CHAPTER TEN

Better Late Than Never:

Life Goes On   154

CHAPTER ELEVEN

Projects and Pastimes:

What Beardstown Ladies Do in

Retirement or Leisure   174

A FEW LAST WORDS   204

APPENDIX A: **Worksheets**   205

APPENDIX B: **Sample Will**   219

RESOURCES WE RECOMMEND   222

GLOSSARY   234

INDEX   249

THE BEARDSTOWN LADIES'
INVESTMENT CLUB

- - - - - - - - - - - - - - - -

Ann Brewer, 61, secretary, charter member.

Ann Corley, 67, retired homemaker, member since 1985.

Doris Edwards, 75, elementary school principal, charter member.

Sylvia Gaushell, 84, retired art teacher, member since 1991.

Shirley Gross, 78, retired medical technologist, charter member.

Margaret Houchins, 54, gift and flower shop owner, member since 1990.

Ruth Huston, 76, retired owner of a dry-cleaning business, charter member.

Carnell Korsmeyer, 68, hog farm owner, member National Pork Board, charter member.

Helen Kramer, 79, retired bank officer, charter member.

Hazel Lindahl, 88, retired medical technician and school nurse, charter member.

Carol McCombs, 46, insurance agency employee, Elsie Scheer's daughter, member since 1993.

Elsie Scheer, 78, retired farmer and teacher's aide, charter member.

Betty Sinnock, 63, bank trust officer, charter member.

Maxine Thomas, 74, retired bank teller, charter member.

Buffy Tillitt-Pratt, 42, real estate broker, member since 1987.

The
Beardstown Ladies'
Stitch-in-Time
Guide to Growing
Your Nest Egg

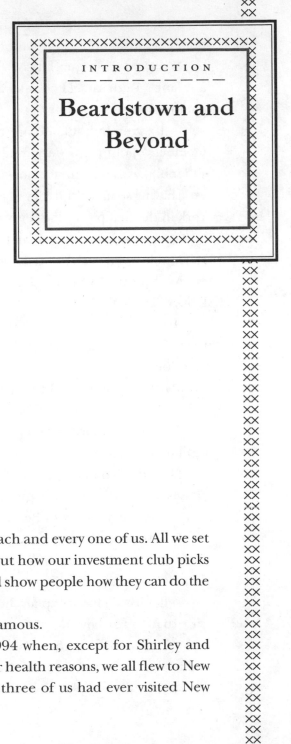

INTRODUCTION

Beardstown and Beyond

It was a complete surprise to each and every one of us. All we set out to do was write a book about how our investment club picks good-quality growth stocks and show people how they can do the same.

All of a sudden, we were famous.

It started in December 1994 when, except for Shirley and Hazel, who remained home for health reasons, we all flew to New York to be on *Donahue*. Only three of us had ever visited New

York (a wonderful place, but where do they learn to drive like that?), and two of us, Ruth and Elsie, had never even flown.

"I'd lived three-quarters of a century and never been on an airplane," Ruth says. "I always wanted to but never thought I'd get the chance."

Just a couple hours before the show, we almost lost three members of our club. Margaret, Carol, and Buffy decided to go shopping, searching for Oakley sunglasses and Polo purses. They were having so much fun they nearly forgot why they were in New York in the first place. Two enormous white limousines were to arrive any minute to take them to *Donahue*! So they jumped in a cab and headed back to the hotel.

As the cab driver raced through the city streets, nothing looked familiar.

"It was hard to communicate," Carol says. "He didn't speak much English, and we were stuffed in the backseat with packages up to our chins."

Margaret told him, "Just take us to Lincoln Center."

"Where?" the cab driver asked.

"Lincoln Center!" Margaret exclaimed. "The cultural arts capital of America!"

As it turned out, we were all on time for *Donahue*—those sunglasses and Polo purses are quite stunning—and the rest is history. At least it's history in Beardstown.

That book showing us on the cover holding a lot of cash, *The Beardstown Ladies' Common-Sense Investment Guide,* has sold more than 300,000 copies and spent 11 weeks on the *New York Times* best-seller list. In it, we explain how we formed our club in 1983 with 16 members and taught ourselves good, conservative principles for purchasing stocks that we believe will double in value within five years. It's not a get-rich-quick scheme. We pick our stocks carefully and plan to hold them for the long term. We believe that anyone can learn what we learned and do well investing in the stock market. The fact that we are women, all from a small town in the heartland of Illinois, and most of us are senior citizens seemed to get everyone's attention. We don't fit people's usual picture of "investor." But that's what we are.

Over time, the "common sense" we put in the title has borne us out. In the first 11 years, our club averaged a 23.4 percent return on our money, better than nearly all Wall Street experts and a good bit better than the S&P 500. In 1991 we made an eye-popping 59.5 percent return!

We've been written about in newspapers in all 50 states. We've been on TV so much, we get recognized most of the places we go. The program *20/20* did a lengthy report on us, and *CBS This Morning* and Harry Smith had us on for a fifth time. At the end of the last segment, Betty smiled at the camera and said, "Good morning, America!" Oops. (Sorry, Harry!)

Of course, we believe this is why people seem to be so interested in us. We're not trained investment experts, and we're certainly not TV personalities. We're the ladies next door. And the past year surely has, as Betty says, "taken us into another dimension. Everything has gone so nicely for us, we're certain the Man upstairs has had a lot to do with it."

Part of being authors, we've found, is getting an incredible amount of mail. We all get lots of letters, but Maxine probably gets the most. When Maxine got home after the first two-week book tour, the post office had 127 letters waiting for her. Her friendliness appeals to people. So far, in all our travels, she has received five marriage proposals. "I just tell them, 'Thank you, but I'm really not interested,' " Maxine says. "But I do like getting them."

Lots of mail just gets sent to "Beardstown Ladies—Beardstown, Illinois." Some of them have funny addresses. One said,

"Famous Investors Known as the Beardstown Ladies." Another said: "Smart Ladies League." The post office takes most of the mail to the Beardstown Chamber of Commerce, where our friend Donna helps sort it.

One of the most interesting things we've noticed since this all started is that ties reach out from our little town to all parts of the country. Carnell says, "Beardstown reaches beyond Beardstown." We hadn't thought of it that way before, but it does.

For instance, Carnell received a letter from a young girl in Iowa who read the book and noticed that Carnell was born the same year as her father. He had gone to high school in Beardstown, but was killed in an accident more than 20 years ago. The girl had lost touch with her roots here. She wanted to know if Carnell had known her dad when he was growing up.

"Of course I did," Carnell told the young woman. "I went to wiener roasts and hay rides at your grandparents' farm."

Dusting off these old associations reveals what we feel is the true value of fame.

Another part of fame is that we're just plain busier than we've ever been in our lives. As Senior Partner this past year, Margaret has been in charge of keeping our schedule. Her calendar looks like an old crossword puzzle: There's something written in every square. Every weekend we go off in two or three groups to book singings, seminars, speeches, or other educational presentations. When we can, we like to travel together, especially to book signings.

Probably the most exciting time we've had was when Betty, Maxine, Carnell, Buffy, and Margaret traveled to Phoenix as special guests for Tony Robbins's "Financial Mastery" seminar. "There were 1,200 people there, including financial pros, paying a lot of money for this information on how to make more money," Margaret says, "and Tony Robbins personally invited us to come and tell our story."

When the presentation was over, the entire audience stood on top of their chairs and wildly cheered our members. "It was the absolute highlight for me," Buffy says. "Now I know how Garth Brooks feels."

Three of us know how it feels to be touring authors. For three weeks Maxine and Betty trooped across the entire country talking into television cameras, microphones, and notebooks about our book. Several weeks later Carnell and Betty went on the road again.

Maxine and Betty visited New York, Cleveland, Milwaukee, Houston, Dallas, Chicago, Phoenix, Denver, Seattle, and Los Angeles, and gave an average of seven interviews per day. Their days began at 6:30 in the morning and didn't end until they had hopped a 7 or 8 P.M. flight to the next town, arriving at their hotel at 10:30 or 11 at night. One night it was after midnight. Their flights were usually after the dinner hour. "We ate a lot of peanuts," Betty says. "Our next book should be on nutrition or stress."

So much for glamour. But seriously, the media has treated us very well. "All my experiences have given me a new respect for the media," Betty says. "We're impressed by how producers, broadcasters, and writers condense what it's taken us years to learn into just a couple minutes of air time or a few paragraphs in the newspaper."

"Of course, they always want to know if we have disagreements," Ann Corley says. "The truth is, since all this happened, we see each other more often. The fellowship is wonderful. If anything, we're closer. We're almost like family."

Another question we're asked is whether it's been hard on

the people around us. Our families have been very supportive. Carnell's daughter threw a *Donahue*-watching party in Fort Wayne. Shirley's son, a well-known geologist, was introduced at a scientific talk as "a relative of the Beardstown Ladies." Ann Brewer's son had us over to Evansville, where we gave a presentation before 400 people.

In fact, teaching people about saving—especially young people—is something we all enjoy. At St. John's Lutheran School, where Elsie attends a Bible class, a sixth-grade boy named Chris has adopted her as his financial mentor.

"He saw us on the *20/20* show," Elsie says. "The next day he asked me many questions. I gave him some material, and now we often talk about investing. He has spina bifida, but he doesn't let things hold him back. He's very intelligent, and he's looking ahead to investing on his own."

We want to help others like Chris learn how to look ahead and prepare for the future. This book came about because, as we traveled around the country talking to people, so many asked us how we grew our own nest eggs and what they could be doing to be ready for retirement.

> *So many people are in the same boat as Bill and me: approaching 50 and feeling the competing needs of helping our children complete their educations and preparing for our own retirement.*
>
> **—Carol McCombs**

Most of us have either retired or are nearing retirement age, and we have all worked toward being financially prepared. That's not to say we have skimped or led lavish lifestyles. On the contrary, we continue to be as careful with our money these days as we've always been, maybe more so. Financial security is something we never take for granted. But, thankfully, we are all comfortable, stable, and secure, and those are nice feelings to have at any age.

We don't treat saving as if it is just for retirement. We have saved for many other goals, as well. Most of us helped pay for our children's and grandchildren's college educations, and even those of our nieces and nephews. We save to invest in businesses. We save so that we can take trips of which we've dreamed for many years. And we save for things that can't be anticipated—whether it is a calamity or a once-in-a-lifetime opportunity. You could say saving is part of our nature.

Don't think that our financial stability at this stage in our lives is because of our recent success. Some of us were already retired before the investment club was formed, and we were not dependent on just our Social Security benefits. We had other investments, which have grown with the knowledge we've gotten from the club.

Although we all have certain things in common, we've traveled many different roads to get here. Some of us invested in family businesses. Others put money away through pension plans. Most of us purchased insurance. Quite a few of us bought government bonds. And we all had basic savings accounts into which we deposited regular amounts on a regular basis. Oddly enough, none of us made a practice of investing in the stock market until we were older, although in hindsight we sure wish we had.

The common principle in all our savings plans was that we learned this lesson: Pay yourself first.

That is the foundation of this book. We all learned—most of us at a very young age—to pay ourselves first by saving something each time we received income. It doesn't matter whether it comes from a paycheck, a gift, a dividend, a tax return, or money found in the street. It doesn't matter whether it's a whopper of a piece of income or a tiny bit. A portion should be put aside before you do anything else with that money, even pay bills.

We were amazed to learn that more than half of all Americans are not saving for their retirements. We've used many proverbs and adages in writing this book, good old common-sense wisdom, but none is more true than this: The day always comes when it's time to pay the piper.

The years *do* fly by. It's easy to think there is all the time in the world when you are busy raising children, achieving career goals, just getting from Monday to Friday. It might seem like the time to start saving is right around the corner, but what we've found is that the time to start saving is *now*.

The common sense we've picked up through our lives has helped us become successful investors and, as we hope to show in this new book, learn how to plan for those Golden Years and save, as well. Of course, many people find it easier not to think about it, and each of us has friends who took that course. They even enjoyed some things in their middle years that we chose to pass up. Their retirements are not as secure as they would like them to be, however, and they have said to us, "If only we had listened back then . . ."

The lessons in this book are for folks who are ready to listen now.

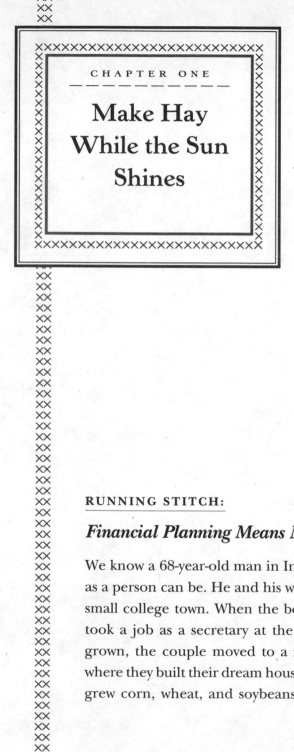

CHAPTER ONE

Make Hay While the Sun Shines

RUNNING STITCH:

Financial Planning Means Many Different Things

We know a 68-year-old man in Indiana who is about as content as a person can be. He and his wife had two sons and lived in a small college town. When the boys started school, the woman took a job as a secretary at the college. Once the boys were grown, the couple moved to a farm a few miles out of town where they built their dream house. They kept their jobs and also grew corn, wheat, and soybeans. Now they're both "retired."

They're on their way to Hawaii, then will visit with their grand-children on the East Coast. They'll be home in time to put in the spring crops, organize the annual church picnic, and meet friends for dinner in Indianapolis. Last winter they redecorated, replacing two couches and all the carpeting. They've been able to help both sons with everything from buying a house, to set-ting up a law firm, to paying for private school tuition. They are really enjoying themselves.

Not bad for a milkman and a secretary. How did they do it? Two little words: financial planning.

They knew from the start what they wanted: a simple, com-fortable lifestyle; to be free of debt; to someday own a farm; to college-educate their sons; and to be near their large, extended family. They worked hard and saved a lot. They didn't smoke, drink, or go on elaborate vacations. They always paid cash in-stead of using credit cards. He stayed with the same dairy com-pany throughout his working life, so he built up a sizable pension. Because she worked at the college, she not only had a good pension, but their sons were able to attend this excellent school free of charge thanks to a tuition remission plan for em-ployees. After they moved to the farm, they continued working another 15 years, both at their jobs and on the farm, socking away even more money in interest-bearing accounts.

It's true they had a lot going for them besides good planning. They stayed married, for one thing. Nothing wreaks more havoc on finances than a divorce. But they had their share of chal-lenges, too. One day the man fell out of his barn 20 feet onto a concrete floor, hurting himself so badly he had to be hospital-ized. But because he was in such good physical shape, he recov-ered almost completely. And because he was in such good financial shape, his bank account didn't suffer too much, either.

The First Step

When you hear the words "financial planning," do you imagine reading a prospectus or hauling out your calculator? We bet you'd much rather take another sip of lemonade and gaze fondly at your savings account passbook. But financial planning involves figuring out what your goals are and then taking the most direct of all possible routes to reach them. Financial planning can be the way to retire early enough to spend 30 years playing golf, or it might mean figuring out how to buy a house, send your kids to college, and still be able to take a vacation.

It doesn't mean you can't work around whatever life throws your way. It does mean you have to have a certain amount of knowledge: mainly knowledge of yourself and what you want. In fact, the very first step in planning your financial future has nothing to do with money. We don't want you to calculate how much you have, how much you make now, how much you think you'll need eventually. Instead, relax. Maybe sit down with a cup of coffee, tea, soda, whatever you like to have while

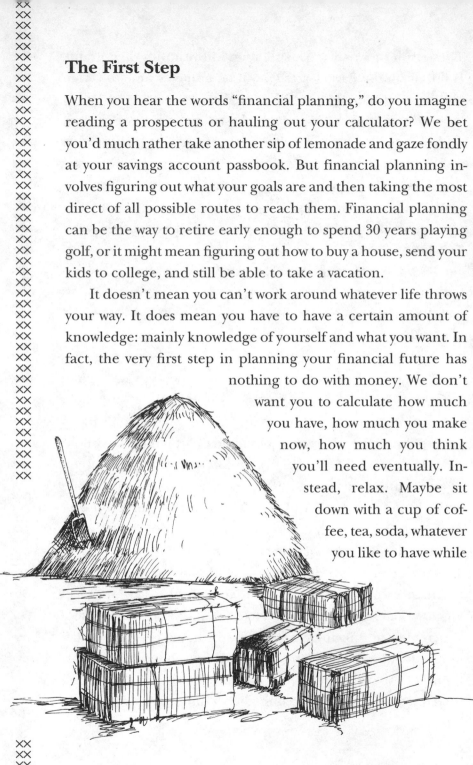

you daydream. If you're married, invite your spouse to join you. It doesn't have to be a big red-circled date on your calendar. Make it a more casual get-together. In fact, it might take more than one session. Maybe you can talk while you take a walk or while you're driving somewhere—wherever you are most comfortable.

Once you're in the right frame of mind, picture yourself five, 10, or 20 years down the road. What are you doing? Are your children in nursery school? College? Or still in high school? Are they living with you or out on their own? Do you want to be available to baby-sit for your grandkids, or would you rather be too busy volunteering at a hospital? Are you traveling around the country in a mobile home? Are you still working because you love your job so much you never want to retire? Do you have a hobby you like? Have you turned it into a part-time career?

As you answer these kinds of questions, take your time. Be leisurely. You probably won't know everything right away. Even if you think you have all the answers, the best-laid plans often need to be changed. It's impossible to predict the future. You can't know whether you'll stay married forever or suddenly be widowed. You can't know how many children you're going to have or whether you'll be rich in health but poor in wealth. That's why it can be hard to think about the future, especially if you're still on the young side, relatively speaking.

Sometimes it's easier to visualize what's dear to your heart. Have you always longed for a window over your kitchen sink? Or a place to watch the sunset? So many people seem not to realize what is really important in their lives as they scurry around trying to get through each day. But clarifying that the window or the sunset is important to you is the first step in figuring out how to get there from here. You can't put a price on something you don't realize you want.

Shirley Gross set a goal 20 years ago to educate her five grandchildren. "I did it a little bit at a time," says Shirley, "using the same principles we now use in the club. I was conservative. I did my homework. I shopped around. One time I bought an eight-year CD with 14 percent interest. That's a great amount considering there is no risk. Three of those grandkids are in college now, one is graduated, and one is a junior in high school."

A little planning now will go a long way toward helping you have more choices later. The important point is to get the process going, to start realizing what makes you want to get up each morning.

Not that we all have followed this advice. Betty Sinnock admits, "I don't think my husband and I ever sat down and approached it quite like that. I know the first rule of thumb is to set your goals. We probably have done it backward in attempting to build a savings plan as well as investing in every retirement plan available to us. The result is that we are in good financial shape. Bob is already retired, and I could retire tomorrow if I wanted to. It's a great relief when you know you could."

On the other hand, not everybody wants to retire. "I thought I was going to retire two years ago," says Betty. "When the time came I decided I wasn't ready. Not only did I want to build that nest egg a little further, but I enjoy being with people I like and doing what I like."

What Is Retirement?

The whole notion of retirement has been changing during the last few decades. It used to be that a person worked for the same company for 40 years, built up a healthy pension, and then, at exactly age 65, stopped working and started . . . well, whatever it was he or she had been dreaming of doing during those 40 years. Nowadays, careers aren't nearly so cut and dried, and retirement is whatever you wind up doing after you've raised your children or gotten to a certain age. It's become another stage of life.

Downsizing and layoffs mean you can't always count on working until you're 65—at least not in the same job. There's also a sense of freedom that means someone might quit at 45 to sail around the world or go back to school. Switching careers—from teaching to selling computers, for example—has become commonplace. Couples are having babies 20 years later than their parents did, and that puts a different spin on the retirement cycle. So the definition of retirement is a lot more fluid and less limiting than it used to be.

A very smart man we know started at the age of 20 working in his father's business. He enjoyed his work so much that he didn't really have any hobbies. He did not believe that the day he turned 65 he would suddenly lose all his interest, expertise, and energy, so he saw no reason to retire according to a birthday. Instead, he gradually, over a period of years and years, shifted his work week. He started teaching at a college one day each week and going into his office the other four days. After a couple of years, he added another day of teaching. A few years after that, he gave himself one day a week to work at home. Next he stopped going into the office, staying in touch by phone and fax. It was such a gentle transition that by the time he and his wife moved to the home they had built on a lake, he was ready to "retire" financially, emotionally, and physically.

The same happily retired man also believes people should *start* working while still in high school. Buffy Tillitt-Pratt does him one better. "I was thinking about retirement before I started working," she says. "When I was in high school, my dad was in his 60s and getting ready to retire. He was the Ford dealer in Beardstown. If he would have held onto the business a couple more years, I think he would have seen that it was something I could have gone in to. Looking back, I would have liked very much to be the Ford dealer in town.

"But since I saw my parents retire successfully while I was still young, I've always been very financially grounded. My plan was to retire at 50. I wanted to have a cabin in Colorado—because my husband loves to hunt—and have a mobile home in Florida for the winter.

"Everything was on pace to accomplish this goal. Then two years ago, just as I turned 40, my son T.J. came along and revised the plan. I don't think we should move him around to accommodate our early retirement, so we plan to stay here until he's through high school. Since I had him so late in life, I will be turning the right age to withdraw my IRA about the time he would need the money for college. Also, I want to continue my real estate business until I know whether he'd be interested in someday taking it over. Delaying retirement 10 years doesn't seem like that big a deal."

Financial Planning Can Be Fun

In Minnesota, two sisters used to spend hours in a boat on a pond that was filled with waterlilies. As they floated slowly through the lily pads, they'd talk about what they wanted to do when they grew up, what sort of house they'd live in, how many children they'd have. Now that they're adults, they use the phrase "lily padding" to mean that sort of easygoing planning.

After we've finished lily padding, we believe in writing things down, or what we call "yellow padding." Somehow putting our thoughts on paper seems to clarify what we've been thinking right along. This is the time to get out the notebook, legal pad, or whatever you prefer. Again, don't even think about the cost of your desires . . . yet. Include things that might not cost a cent. Start by listing your "life" goals. A financial plan-ner can't help you with this. Only you know your-self well enough to be realistic and honest.

Do you want to be the most successful busi-nessperson you know? The best Sunday school teacher? Do you want to impress your neighbors, your mother-in-law, or your best friend? Is money more important to you than education or vice

> *My retirement plan, though it has changed in form and substance, has been a long time in the making.*
> —**Carnell Korsmeyer**

versa? Would you rather have an MD or an MBA? Do you want to write a book, design a garden, or raise show horses? Are you a city person or a country lover? Are you happiest volunteering for your local homeless shelter or making a lot of money to do-nate to charity?

The answers to these kinds of questions affect how much you make and, in turn, your financial plan. Being mindful of your personal values will help you make decisions when it comes to the second list: your wish list. This should include everything you might want that does cost money. And we mean *everything*. You're still not even thinking about how you'll possibly afford it. You're just making a list.

In no particular order, write down what you want under a column marked something like "Wish List." Mark the next col-umn "When." This is where you'll put a general date for when you want whatever it is you're wishing for. A trip around the world, for instance, might be slated for the year 2005. A new car might be next spring.

Now you have your all-time best wish list. If you're a simple, modest person, it's probably a simple, modest list. If you're a grand schemer and dreamer, it's probably outrageous. Either way, now that you have a clear picture of your imaginary Paradise, the next step is to consider what it will take to turn those wishes into reality. That's what the third column on your sheet of paper is for. Under "Cost," write down a guess of what each item will cost. Don't worry about under- or overestimating. This is a rough blueprint, not exact architectural plans.

Now the trick is to turn each line—the goal, the timetable, and the cost—into action.

Maybe one of your goals is to send your three children to the top private colleges in the country. When you calculate the cost (a conservative $300,000) and the timetable (within the next 10 years), you realize that you'll need to change careers, work four jobs, live in a tent—or all of the above. You rethink your goal and decide that your children are bright enough to do well at one of the very good public universities. The timetable is the same, but the cost drops by $200,000. You get to keep living in a house after all.

Once you've gone through each item on your wish list, you'll have a sense of how much money you'll need, when you'll need it, and what you'll have to do to come up with it. In other words, you'll have a financial plan.

Well, you'll have half a financial plan. To your wish list, you need to add a "necessary" list. This is the no-frills part of the plan and includes health insurance, disability insurance, life insurance, and debt repayment. Most people will have the cost of owning a home, college education, and retirement on this part of the list, too. It's just a lot more fun to think about all those special wishes and dreams first.

Down to Brass Tacks

A financial plan is not set in stone. It's meant to be played with and continually adjusted. As your circumstances change, so, too, will your financial plan. It's like having a piece of clay. If you make a vase out of the clay, paint it with blue glaze, and then fire it in a kiln, you'll have a beautiful blue vase forever. Or you can keep sculpting the clay into different shapes to please yourself and match your mood. When you're 25, you might want a shiny new car. When you're 55, you might prefer a shiny new kitchen. If you're single, you may want to make early retirement your main goal. If you have children, maybe saving for your grand-children's education takes precedence.

The important point is that we all need a financial plan. And we all need money to put the plan into action. But how much money? That's the key question. Our goals remain too vague and we won't get around to saving for them until we can estimate how much they will cost. And that's true for those at any income level.

Carol McCombs says, "Bill and I have not really sat down to look at the Big Question: Are we saving enough to retire the way we want to and when we want to? That investigation will be coming soon, I'm sure. We've talked about getting a motor home and traveling the country. But we'll probably wind up right here cutting the grass."

What they need—what we all need—is a way of figuring how long our retirement will last and how much money it will take. The tools you need to do this include several tables, worksheets, and statistics. Combined, they will give you a good approximation of how many years you need to provide for and how much it will cost. Then you also will have a realistic age to aim for retirement. First, take a look at the life expectancy chart.

No chart can guarantee how long you will live, but it can give you a plausible scenario. Keep in mind that because of the way in which this table was calculated, you have a 50 percent chance of living longer or dying sooner. Most financial experts tell you to tack on at least five years to these figures to be on the safe side. Then, if it's not too hard for you to think about your own life span, weigh other factors, such as how long your parents and grandparents lived, your overall health, and any risks.

In Maxine Thomas's case, it was not a rosy picture she saw growing up. "My mother died when I was 10," Maxine recalls. "She left no life insurance because this was in the days when responsibility was all on the men. My daddy went blind from glaucoma not long after that. He was old and stubborn, and very bitter about his blindness.

"So my husband and I planned well for our retirement. Of course, what you plan for and what actually happens can be two different things. Some things you can never fully plan for, such as the death of a spouse. But being financially prepared is one less thing to worry about in a time of crisis."

As Aunt Margaret used to say, "Hope for the best, but be prepared for the worst."

Let's say you're 50 years old now. If you decide to retire at 55, you'll need to have enough to live on for at least 30 years. Sounds like a long time, doesn't it? If you wait until you're 70, you'll only need enough for about 16 years. Not only that, but you'll be contributing to a retirement fund for 15 additional years, which adds up to more money spread over fewer years. So, if you love your job, count yourself among the blessed and keep on working.

Table 1.2 gives you a very rough idea of how much you need to save each year for your retirement, depending on your age

Table 1.1: How Long You Can Expect to Live

Age	Years	Age	Years	Age	Years
10	71.7	40	42.5	70	16.0
11	70.7	41	41.5	71	15.3
12	69.7	42	40.6	72	14.6
13	68.8	43	39.6	73	13.9
14	67.8	44	38.7	74	13.2
15	66.8	45	37.7	75	12.5
16	65.8	46	36.8	76	11.9
17	64.8	47	35.9	77	11.2
18	63.9	48	34.9	78	10.6
19	62.9	49	34.0	79	10.0
20	61.9	50	33.1	80	9.5
21	60.9	51	32.2	81	8.9
22	59.9	52	31.3	82	8.4
23	59.0	53	30.0	83	7.9
24	58.0	54	29.5	84	7.4
25	57.0	55	28.6	85	6.9
26	56.0	56	27.7	86	6.5
27	55.1	57	26.8	87	6.1
28	54.1	58	25.9	88	5.7
29	53.1	59	25.0	89	5.3
30	52.2	60	24.2	90	5.0
31	51.2	61	23.3	91	4.7
32	50.2	62	22.5	92	4.4
33	49.3	63	21.6	93	4.1
34	48.3	64	20.8	94	3.9
35	47.3	65	20.0	95	3.7
36	46.4	66	19.2	96	3.4
37	45.4	67	18.4	97	3.2
38	44.4	68	17.6	98	3.0
39	43.5	69	16.8	99	2.8

YOU CAN EXPECT TO LIVE THIS MANY MORE YEARS

Source: Internal Revenue Service

and income. (To calculate a more exact amount, see the Retirement Planner worksheet on page 206 in Appendix A.)

The shorthand version here applies to a working couple who will qualify for Social Security. (We'll go into that in Chapter 3.)

Table 1.2: How Much You Need to Save Annually for Retirement

Look under the current age column and find the line nearest to how old you are now. Now go across to find how much you make a year. The amount where your current age and current salary intersect is how much you need to be saving each year until you reach retirement.

	CURRENT SALARY		
CURRENT AGE	**$35,000**	**$50,000**	**$75,000**
30 years old	$4,035	$6,602	$11,511
40 years old	$6,520	$10,644	$18,425
50 years old	$11,420	$18,904	$32,349

It assumes they will receive an 8 percent return on investments and that they want to retire at age 65. It factors in a 4 percent inflation rate, but does not take into account raises or any investments they already have. If they save according to this chart, they will be able to live on 75 percent of their preretirement income, which is a bit on the low side. Many experts use 80 percent as a more realistic rule of thumb, but we've also seen some use 70 percent. Again, no matter which percentage you use, you'll get an *estimate*, not an *exactimate*.

You can see right away from this chart that the younger you are and the sooner you start, the less you need to save each year.

We'll say it again and again: *Start saving now.* No matter how little you can spare—or think you can spare—you won't be sorry if you save sooner rather than later.

As Carnell Korsmeyer puts it, "Beardstown is river country so we are mindful of river lore. I remember a quote that goes, 'On a river you can't simply do nothing, there is no standing still.' If you don't go someplace the river will take you some other place, usually undesirable. That's how my husband and I feel about retirement and our financial future. We best not 'do nothing,' or life might not take us where we want to go."

Inflation

Planning our financial future reminds us of the "Fortunately, Unfortunately" stories. Have you ever heard one? They go this way: Fortunately, you earn a decent living. Unfortunately, you don't want to keep working forever. Fortunately, you have saved for years so you can retire. Unfortunately, there is a little matter of inflation . . .

There are two ways of looking at inflation, so we have two different tables. One method is to think of inflation as how much *less* our money will buy us in the future. In Table 1.3 you'll see that after 10 years at a 4 percent inflation rate—a probable average rate for the next several decades—your $100 will get you as much as $67 will buy you today.

A second approach is to think of inflation as how much *more* money we will need in the future to maintain ourselves in the style to which we've grown accustomed. Look over Table 1.4.

Using the same example, if you spend $100 today, in 10 years you would have to spend $148 for the same item. It's easy to see inflation can be a big retirement budget buster.

Table 1.3: How Inflation Affects Savings

Let's say you want to find out how much you savings will be worth in 20 years. Look down the column on the left and find your 20-year line. Now pick a probable inflation rate for the next 20 years. If you choose 6 percent, you would see that where 20 years and 6 percent intersect the number is $31. That means that in 20 years, every $100 you have now would be worth only $31.

	INFLATION RATE FOR $100			
IN THIS NUMBER OF YEARS	4%	6%	8%	10%
5	$82	$75	$68	$62
10	69	56	46	39
15	59	42	32	24
20	52	31	21	15
25	44	23	15	9
30	35	17	10	6

Table 1.4: Another Way to Look At Inflation

Use this chart the same way as Table 1.3. But the amount you find at the intersection of the inflation rate and the number of years will tell you how much you would have to spend in future dollars to buy what today's $100 will get you.

	INFLATION RATE FOR $100			
IN THIS NUMBER OF YEARS	4%	6%	8%	10%
5	$122	$134	$147	$161
10	$148	$179	$216	$259
15	$180	$240	$317	$418
20	$219	$321	$466	$673
25	$267	$429	$685	$1,084
30	$324	$574	$1,006	$1,745

Although the power of compound interest can be even stronger than that bully inflation, you might not understand how compound interest can protect you.

Fortunately, our next chapter happens to be about the magic of compound interest.

Finishing Stitch

1. WRITE DOWN WHAT YOU WANT OUT OF LIFE.

2. FIGURE OUT HOW MUCH IT WILL COST.

3. MAKE A FINANCIAL PLAN TO ACHIEVE YOUR GOALS.

4. START SAVING.

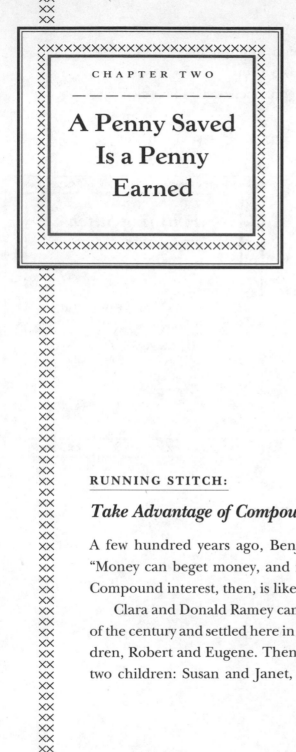

CHAPTER TWO

A Penny Saved Is a Penny Earned

RUNNING STITCH:

Take Advantage of Compound Interest

A few hundred years ago, Benjamin Franklin put it simply: "Money can beget money, and its offspring can beget more." Compound interest, then, is like a family tree.

Clara and Donald Ramey came to America around the turn of the century and settled here in Beardstown. They had two children, Robert and Eugene. Then Robert and Eugene each had two children: Susan and Janet, Irene and Walter. Now there were eight members of the family. That might not sound like a lot, but watch what happens over a bit more time, as the family keeps reproducing.

Susan has two children, Elbert and Dorothy; Janet has two children, Albert and William; Irene has two children, John and Charles; and Walter has two children, Martha and Hannah.

Next, each of these offspring has just two children. Elbert has Anna and Lucretia; Dorothy has Joel and Jean; Albert has Anna Louise and Belle; William has Lawrence and Mathilde; John has Emma and Dorothy Anne; Charles has Susan and Elizabeth; Martha has John, Jr., and William II; and Hannah has Stephen and Henry. The Ramey family now numbers 32 within four generations.

Within two more generations, this clan contains more than 100 members, and the great-grandmother is complaining she can't get them all to come to family reunions. All because Clara and Donald had two children. And their children had children . . .

What if we substitute today's money for tomorrow's offspring? If Carol, who is 40 years old, starts to save $50 a month in an 8 percent monthly interest account, this is how much she'll have at various ages:

- When she's 50: $9,147
- When she's 60: $29,451
- When she's 70: $74,518

The interest alone accounts for $56,518 of her total at the age of 70.

Now look what happens if she could squeeze $150 out of her budget each month:

- When she's 50: $27,442
- When she's 60: $88,353
- When she's 70: $223,554

In this case, the interest accounts for $169,554—more than three-fourths of the total. Hard to believe a little bit of interest makes such a big difference, isn't it? No wonder when asked what his most important discovery was, intellectual giant Albert Einstein is said to have answered: "Compound interest." There *is* a mathematical formula for calculating interest rates. If you're a math whiz, you might like to play with it:

$$A = P(1 + r)t$$

where A = the amount of money you'll have at the end of a period of time; P = principal; r = rate of interest; and t = time period.

So, if you invest $1,000 in something that yields 6 percent compounded annually, in five years you'd have $1,338:

$$A = 1000 (1 + .06)^5$$
$$A = 1000 (1.06)^5$$
$$A = 1000 (1.06 \times 1.06 \times 1.06 \times 1.06 \times 1.06)$$
$$A = 1338$$

Compound interest calculators and computer programs are available, not to mention friendly bankers who can give you bottom-line numbers. Luckily for us, compound interest is much easier to understand than the theory of relativity.

Start with simple interest. You probably understand simple interest pretty well. You put $100 in a 5 percent savings account.

After a year you have $105. After two years you have $110. After three years you have $115. Only your original $100 earns interest.

But simple interest won't get you very far on the road to riches. The best way to reach the retirement goals you set for yourself in the last chapter is to take advantage of compound interest. What do we mean by that?

The Magic of Compound Interest

Compound interest means *all* the money invested earns interest. Then the *combined* amount of the original investment and its interest earns *more* interest. So $100 in an account with a 5 percent return *compounded* annually would give you $105 the first year. But the second year, you'd earn 5 percent of $105—not just of $100. Your investment would now be worth $110.25. The third year, you'd earn 5 percent on $110.25 and have a total of $115.76. While the difference in this example is only pennies, the longer the money stays invested, the more the money is working for you, earning all that interest. After a few more years, the difference is dramatic.

The Beardstown Ladies' Common-Sense Investment Guide describes how we applied this same idea to the stock market with such success. Month in and month out, each of us contributes $25 to the club . . . and lets it stay there to grow through the magic of compound interest. At last count, our original $100 investment had grown substantially, through additional contributions, dividends, and interest.

We've had comparable success as individual investors, thanks to compound interest. For example, our club's broker, Homer Rieken, recommended a mutual fund investment to Shirley for her grandchildren. After looking at Table 2.1 and Figures 2.1 and 2.2, you can see why Shirley was convinced it was a great idea.

TABLE 2.1: TEMPLETON WORLD FUND
HYPOTHETICAL $2,000 INITIAL INVESTMENT

Year	Price/Share	# of Shares	$Value
7/1/80	$15.92*	118	$1,885
12/31/80	17.60*	122	2,144
12/31/81	17.35	131	2,277
12/31/82	19.75	138	2,718
12/31/83	12.32	296	3,642
12/31/84	11.51	331	3,815
12/31/85	14.06	357	5,018
12/31/86	14.74	400	5,890
12/31/87	12.66	481	6,091
12/31/88	14.16	515	7,291
12/31/89	16.28	549	8,938
12/31/90	12.41	606	7,517
12/31/91	14.27	684	9,755
12/31/92	13.06	771	10,072
12/31/93	15.71	857	13,457
12/31/94	14.17	958	13,575
6/30/95	16.10	958	15,424

* Price adjusted for stock split 3/31/83 for purpose of comparison

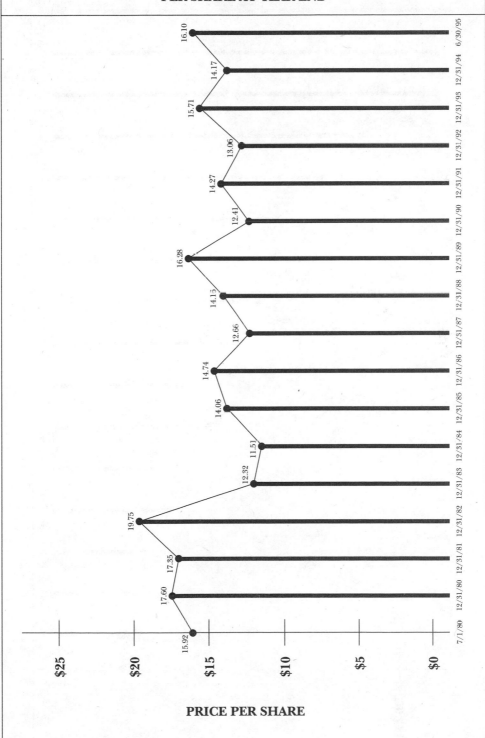

FIGURE 2.1: TEMPLETON WORLD FUND PRICE PER SHARE AT YEAR END

PRICE PER SHARE

YEAR

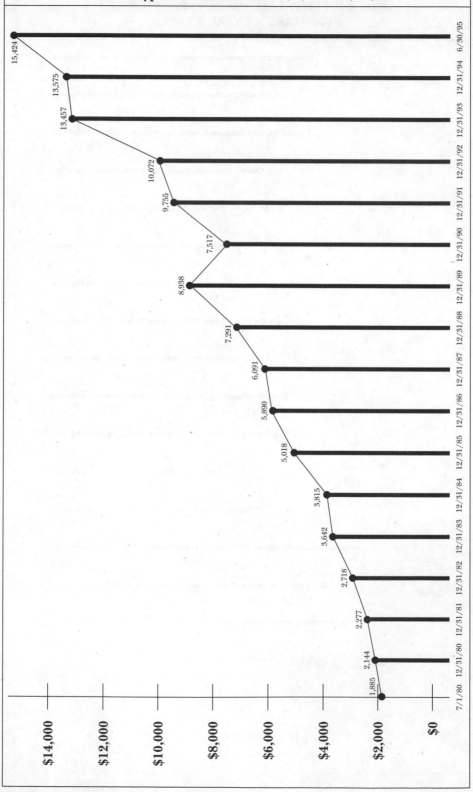

FIGURE 2.2: TEMPLETON WORLD FUND
$2,000 Hypothetical Investment 7/1/80 — 6/30/95

ANOTHER EXAMPLE

Imagine your twins, Tom and Terry, are bitten by the savings bug at an early age. By the time they're eight years old, they both start saving part of their allowance every month. Tom puts all his money in a giant blue crayon piggy bank. His twin sister, Terry, has long conversations with her grandfather, a great believer in the stock market. With his help, she invests her money in a common stock company.

They each save $5 a month for the next 25 years. Meanwhile, they marry and want to buy their first homes at the same time. When Tom and his wife empty the proverbial piggy bank, they find $1,500. Not bad for such a small monthly investment—but only enough to rent an apartment.

Terry and her husband are delighted to discover that her stock is now worth $7,357—just enough for a down payment on the house they want.

This is more than sibling rivalry at work: It's compound interest. You put money in an interest-bearing account and the money earns interest, then the interest itself starts earning interest. It's a shame that a concept so simple—and rewarding— is so little understood by many people.

Here's how the twins wound up with such different-size nest eggs:

Tom and his piggy bank:

$5 a month = $60 a year times 25 years = $1,500

Terry and her stock:

$5 a month at an average 10 percent return over 25 years = $7,357

Teach Your Children Well

If you could teach your children only one money lesson, the wonderful way compound interest works would be the most valuable. "My advice," Margaret Houchins says, "is start them young. Don't let your kids get the idea that there isn't any left over for saving.

"I recently went home to Kansas City, where I have four grandchildren. I told my kids that now is the time to get these young ones accustomed to putting money away. Three of them are teenagers, and that's plenty old enough to understand the basics—like the miracle of compound interest and the importance of paying yourself first. I didn't have access to this information when I was young. When saving and investing are not part of your way of doing things growing up, it's hard to change later in life.

"One of my grandchildren is just a year old. If we can begin a savings program for her, she could have $100,000 tucked away by the time she gets married."

If your children can't relate to this example, here's a fairy tale they'll love: Imagine you start your investment program with exactly one penny. Then you have the good fortune to find an investment that provides 100 percent interest every day. How much will you have in one month? With an initial investment of one cent, you guess not very much, right?

The second day, you'd have your penny plus interest. You'd be up to two cents. One hundred percent of two cents is two cents, so by day three, you'd have four cents. Still small potatoes. But somewhere around the middle of the month, those pennies start piling up at a faster and faster pace.

Within *two weeks,* your penny would be worth more than $300. How much would you earn by the end of a month? Seeing is believing.

More than $5 million, all from compound interest. This example *is* a fairy tale . . . but only because it's impossible to find an investment that will yield 100 percent daily interest. It's easy to find a real investment that yields 10 percent interest, though, and once you do, your money will increase more quickly than you could imagine.

Day 1	$0.01
Day 2	0.02
Day 3	0.04
Day 4	0.08
Day 5	0.16
Day 6	0.32
Day 7	0.64
Day 8	1.28
Day 9	2.56
Day 10	5.12
Day 11	10.24
Day 12	20.48
Day 13	40.96
Day 14	81.92
Day 15	163.84
Day 16	327.68
Day 17	655.36
Day 18	1,310.72
Day 19	2,621.44
Day 20	5,242.88
Day 21	10,485.76
Day 22	20,971.52
Day 23	41,943.04
Day 24	83,886.08
Day 25	167,772.16
Day 26	335,544.32
Day 27	671,088.64
Day 28	1,342,177.28
Day 29	2,684,354.56
Day 30	5,368,709.12

The longer you can let compound interest spin its gold, the better off you'll be. That's because compound interest works by geometric progression. It starts out slowly but gathers momentum as it grows. If you were to plot the penny story on a graph, you'd see a steep upward curve that would look like the one in Figure 2.3.

Dollars and Sense

We think it's so important to understand that a seemingly small difference in monthly savings today makes a great deal of difference in tomorrow's nest egg. If you try to save even $15 instead of $10, in 20 years the difference in earned interest will be enormous.

Carnell's advice is to start early so the money saved has the chance to work longer for you. "It will be there, having grown to larger figures, when you need it," she says. But she adds, "You must put some in today, and every day."

It's probably worth sacrificing a little bit now to be comfortable later on. Especially if

FIGURE 2.3: A PENNY COMPOUNDED

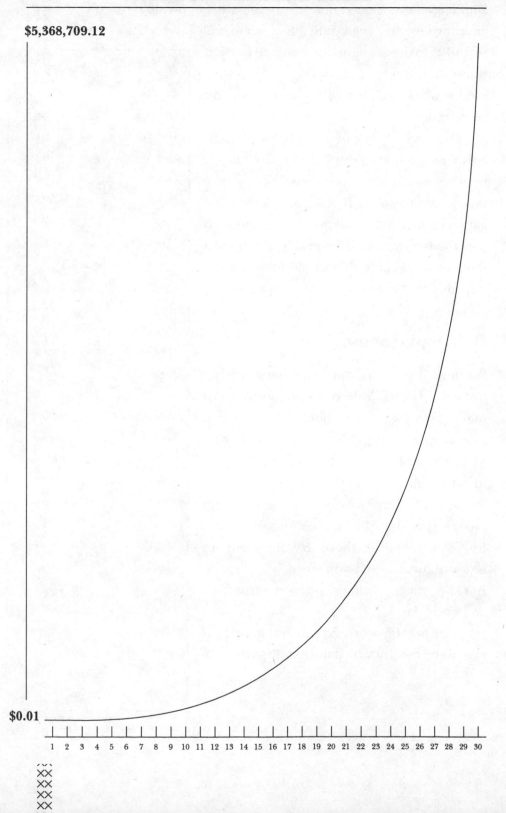

you don't really have to suffer in order to put a few more dollars into an investment. Almost everyone can find painless ways of "finding" money they didn't realize they could save. (In Chapter 4 we'll offer ideas on how to economize in order to invest more.)

At a financial institution in the area, there are several employees in their 20s and many a bit older. Every day one of the older employees brings her own lunch from home—often last night's dinner leftovers, which she heats up in the handy microwave the bank provides. Every day some of the other tellers go out for lunch and spend an average of $4 to $6 dollars each. When she's thirsty, the older woman drinks from the office water cooler. On the rare occasions she goes out to eat, she just drinks water, too. The others buy soda from a machine at 50 cents a pop. The older woman makes coffee at home for a Thermos she brings to work; the others pay 50 cents for coffee in the lounge.

How much of a difference can bringing your lunch from home make? If the other tellers brought their lunches from home—even twice a week—they'd save at least $40 a month. Doesn't sound like much? Wait. If they drank water and brought their own coffee, they'd save an additional $30 a month. In 40 years, right around the time they'd like to retire, that amount— $70 a month—would grow to $33,600 even without compound interest.

To add insult to injury, the thrifty employee quietly collects all those soda cans, recycles them, and makes $10 a month in deposits. Her nest egg will be $2,400 larger in 20 years, thanks to her carefree co-workers.

From One Small Acorn . . .

Say you've been wise enough to start saving nice and early in life. You're continuing to save as much as you can as often as you can. Is there anything else you could be doing to make your nest egg grow?

First, think about the Ramey family tree again. If each Ramey family member had one more baby—three children instead of two—by the time great-grandmother wanted to have her reunion, she'd have to write 601 more invitations. What does genealogy have to do with retirement planning? Interest rates are a lot like the size of families. How much difference do you think a 6 percent interest rate versus a 7 percent rate would make? You might guess about one-seventh or something like that. In fact, one point of interest can be the difference between living comfortably when you retire . . . or just getting by.

One or two points has a major effect on investments. And the longer the money is invested, the more difference the interest rate makes. This is the strategy we have always applied in our club, since the stock market historically yields a greater return than more conservative investments over long periods.

Let's say you stick with a garden-variety savings account. If you deposit $5,000 in an account that offers 4 percent interest, in 25 years you'll have $13,568. (You'll probably barely break even with inflation, but we'll talk about that in more detail in Chapter 7.)

With a little more risk, you could invest $5,000 in bonds that yield 6 percent. In 25 years you'd have $22,325. If you're willing to take the next step, you'll really reap some rewards. In 25 years the same amount of money in a mutual fund account that yield a 10 percent return, compounded monthly, will give you

$60,285—that's $37,960 (or 170 percent) more because of a 4 percent difference in interest rates.

- $5,000 at 4 percent in 25 years = $13,568
- $5,000 at 6 percent in 25 years = $22,325
- $5,000 at 10 percent in 25 years = $60,285

These examples assume you have a modest amount to invest. What if your great-uncle Henry leaves you an unexpected inheritance of $50,000? If you invested it for 25 years at 6 percent, you could retire with a lovely nest egg of $223,248. If you tried just a bit harder and invested in a 7 percent vehicle, you'd have $286,271. And at 8 percent, your original inheritance could provide $367,008. Can you imagine what you could do with that extra $143,760 those two little percentage points will earn you?

- $50,000 at 6 percent in 25 years = $223,248
- $50,000 at 7 percent in 25 years = $286,271
- $50,000 at 8 percent in 25 years = $367,008

To make up your own scenarios for how your money can work for you, look at Table 2.2. This chart shows you how much money will earn over time and with different interest rates. Careful, though. We've found once you start playing with compound interest, it's hard to stop.

The 2 Percent Solution

Ray, an unmarried credit analyst in Missouri, was making a very good income. Through his job, he had a retirement plan. At the bottom of the statements he received each quarter was a help-

Table 2.2: How Your Money Grows with Compound Interest

IN THIS MANY YEARS	IF YOU INVEST $100 AT THIS INTEREST RATE:								
	4%	5%	6%	7%	8%	9%	10%	11%	12%
1	$104	105	106	107	108	109	110	111	112
2	108	110	112	114	117	119	121	123	125
3	112	116	119	123	126	130	133	137	140
4	117	122	126	131	136	141	146	152	157
5	122	128	134	140	147	154	161	169	176
6	127	134	142	150	159	168	177	187	197
7	132	141	150	161	171	183	195	208	221
8	137	148	159	172	185	199	214	230	248
9	142	155	169	184	200	217	236	256	277
10	148	163	179	197	216	237	259	284	311
11	154	171	190	210	233	258	285	315	348
12	160	180	201	225	252	281	314	350	390
13	167	189	213	241	272	307	345	388	436
14	173	198	226	258	294	334	380	431	489
15	180	208	240	276	317	364	418	478	547
16	187	218	254	295	343	397	459	531	613
17	195	229	269	316	370	433	505	590	687
18	203	241	285	338	400	472	556	654	669
19	211	253	303	362	432	514	612	726	861
20	219	266	321	387	466	560	673	806	964
25	228	279	340	414	503	611	740	879	1,080

ful little reminder of how much income he'd have, based on his current investment, if he were to retire at age 65. The month he turned 40, he looked at the amount on the bottom of the statement, shuddered, and went straight to his financial planner. Ray asked, "What do I have to do now?"

Like any good financial planner, he gave Ray three different scenarios, showing how much Ray would have to save each year to retire at age 55, 60, or 65. It was soon clear that 55 would be next to impossible, 60 would be a real stretch, but 65 would be very easy. If, that is, Ray could save $20,000 *a year* to invest in government bonds that were earning about 7 percent.

Ray shuddered again. Even on his generous salary, he thought it would be impossible to save $20,000. His financial planner showed him what would happen if he simply shifted his savings plan to include more stocks. Using a modest 9 percent return rate, he would need to save $12,000 a year. Breathing a sigh of relief, Ray was able to begin his 40s with a feeling of security while still enjoying $8,000 more a year of the good life.

A Cautionary Tale

Now that you understand the positive power of compound interest, a word of caution. The same magic can turn into sorcery when it comes to credit card bills. A few years ago, a divorced, 65-year-old woman in California was in a car accident. She couldn't continue working as a piano teacher during her long recovery. Without disability insurance, savings, or home equity, she was in a financial bind. Rather than ask her children for help, she decided to live on her credit cards. For one whole year, she charged everything from groceries to gasoline, to the tune of $20,000. It doesn't take a compound interest calculator to figure out that there is not much hope of her paying off even the 18 percent interest, no less the original amount, on this big a debt, at least not within her working life.

While 10 percent interest is considered terrific on an investment, it wouldn't be too terrific for a credit card rate. Yet most credit cards carry at least 18 percent interest. And if by now you believe that money blooms and flourishes at 10 percent, keep in mind that debt grows like a weed gone wild.

There was a couple in Pennsylvania who had always wanted to have a second honeymoon. In fact, they had never had a honeymoon when they were first married. So the husband planned a surprise for his wife: a once-in-a-lifetime trip to Paris. He lined up his parents to watch the kids, checked with his wife's boss to make sure she could get time off, made airline reservations, hotel reservations, and even rented a car. They had a wonderful 10 days sampling café au lait, croissants, and chocolate, stayed in a real castle, looked at beautiful artwork, and of course bought lots of presents for grandparents and children.

That was three years ago. But the wife is still surprised every month when the credit card bill comes. Seems they just don't get anywhere paying down the $5,000 that once-in-a-lifetime trip cost. At least that's how much her husband told her it cost. Once she really studied the bill, she figured out that at 19 percent interest, the trip really had cost them $6,000. If they had invested $5,000 at 10 percent, by now they'd have enough extra to take that trip and go first class all the way.

It's enough to make you want to cut up the little plastic cards today.

But that said, remember that wise men like Franklin and Einstein have praised the power of compound interest when used *wisely*. An even wiser Beardstown Lady remarks, "Take advantage of compound interest."

Finishing Stitch

—————————————

1. START SAVING EARLY.

2. KEEP PUTTING MONEY INTO INVESTMENT ACCOUNTS.

3. FIND THE BEST INTEREST RATES.

4. PAY CREDIT CARD BALANCES MONTHLY.

5. KEEP SAVING.

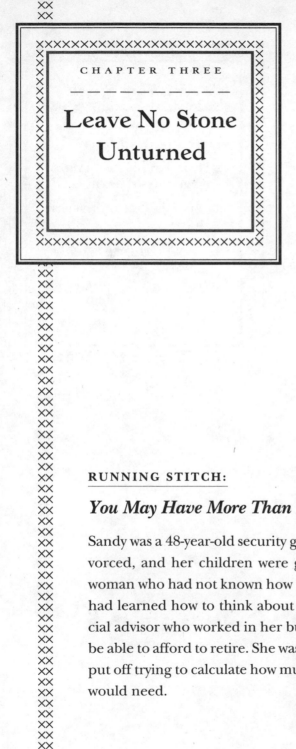

CHAPTER THREE

Leave No Stone Unturned

RUNNING STITCH:

You May Have More Than You Think

Sandy was a 48-year-old security guard in a small city. She was divorced, and her children were grown. A classic example of a woman who had not known how to balance a checkbook, Sandy had learned how to think about money enough to ask a financial advisor who worked in her building if she was ever going to be able to afford to retire. She was so anxious about this, she had put off trying to calculate how much she had and how much she would need.

On a salary of $28,000 a year, she managed to save 15 percent, which she put into a mutual fund. She also owned a little stock in the utility company where her ex-husband worked. So her friend was able to reassure her that if she continued the excellent habits she had begun, she would be able to retire comfortably at 65. A happy ending.

If you want to achieve your dreams, it's helpful to make the most of what you have. And you probably have more than you think you do.

To make the most of compound interest, you need to know how much you have to invest. Most people think they don't have any extra money sitting around. If you think of your financial worth as how much you have in your checking and savings accounts, you probably don't have any left over to invest. Then when you remember that big credit card balance, you might assume your worth was some negative number.

That's why it can seem as if calculating how much you have isn't worth bothering with. But we bet you'll be pleasantly surprised once you plunge in.

Your net worth is figured by first adding up your assets: all your property, stocks, possessions, cash, and money due you by others. Then you count up your liabilities: any amount you are liable or responsible for paying to someone else.

A net worth statement is a personal balance sheet, the value of everything you own or can convert into cash *minus* all the money you owe in bills, debts, loans, or any other expense. A net worth statement is not a budget. (A budget is an action plan for spending each day, week, or month, and we'll talk about that in the next chapter.) The goal is to keep increasing the amount of your assets or investments while reducing the amount of your liabilities or debts. You'll also be able to tell at a glance whether you are saving and investing wisely or charging and spending too well.

Knowing your net worth is the best way to assess how your family would survive a catastrophe and how much insurance coverage you might need. It's a sort of financial thermometer, a reading of where you are right now. If you make a new net worth statement every year or two, you'll have a good sense of whether you're moving up or down, forward or backward. One of the Beardstown Ladies' themes is planning, according to Ann Corley. "Shirley often reminds us of the importance of taking stock of your situation," Ann adds. "If you do not know what your current financial picture is, how can you make intelligent decisions about how to proceed?"

Hazel Lindahl also mentions Shirley when she thinks about net worth. "I'm not like Shirley," Hazel says. "On the first of the year, she makes a careful assessment of her net worth. I've been planning to do that for the last four years but never have. I hate to admit it, but I've always been careless about business matters. I'm grateful I've had an easy life financially. I guess I had a guardian angel who made sure I had what I needed when I needed it."

Sadly, not everyone has such an angel.

A young woman in Texas had never done a net worth statement with her husband. One year on St. Patrick's Day he was diagnosed with cancer. By Easter he had died, leaving her alone with her two small children and not a clue as to their financial situation. She didn't know how much life insurance he had; what kind of pension plan or Social Security benefits; how much they owed on their mortgage; what their boats were worth; the status of a business he owned in Los Angeles; or many other financial details. If only they had worked out a net worth statement before he became ill, she wouldn't have had to deal with such a big task while also coping with her emotional grief.

So the time to begin is today.

Where Do You Begin?

Gather all your financial records together in a place where you can work. Depending on how organized you are, this part of the process may take awhile. That's okay. Don't try to rush yourself. Give yourself a lot of patience and time.

The records you need to gather include checking, savings accounts, money market accounts, stocks, bonds, insurance policies, individual retirement accounts (IRAs), Keoghs, pension plans, real estate, loan notes (for money owed to you), outstanding invoices for work you've done, and appraisal forms or receipts for any valuable possessions.

Once you have these statements and reports in one place, check to make sure you have any telephone numbers you might need for verifying or updating account information. These might include your bank's phone number as well as numbers for your accountant, stock broker, insurance agent, personnel manager, lawyer, or relatives.

Next decide whether you want to keep your net worth statement in a notebook you can update regularly, on a computer, or on a legal pad in a special file. We think a fine way to keep track is to use scratch paper and then fill in the final figures on copies of the Net Worth Statements in this book in Appendix A on pages 208–211. You could photocopy the forms so you can update them whenever you need to.

On the left side of a piece of paper, write down everything you own. This is your assets list. It should include anything you could exchange for cash. You might think this is obvious and easy, but you'll be surprised at what you might miss the first time around. For example, if you still owe a hefty mortgage on your home, do you list your house as an asset? How about your pet poodle? Or your family silver? What if you own a small store? Or a restaurant? Or run a car repair business?

The rule of thumb is to put down absolutely everything this first go-around. Don't worry about giving anything a dollar value yet. The idea is to do a paper roundup of every possible asset you have.

If you could sell your house and make more than you owe the mortgage company, list it. If your pet poodle is a purebred show dog, list it. If your store or car repair business or restaurant could be sold, list it.

On the other hand, if you have an heirloom diamond engagement ring that you'd sooner starve than part with, don't bother listing it as an asset. Assets are those possessions or investments that, in a real financial pinch, you would be willing and able to let go. We hope you never get to the point where you'd have to consider selling your family silver, but if you know in your heart you could do it to house and clothe your children, then go ahead and put down that as an asset. Not only will you know what you're worth, you'll know what's important to you when you've completed this exercise. It's a way of prioritizing your money and your values.

On the right-hand side of the list, you're going to put a dollar amount for each item. Some of these figures will be quite accurate and specific. It's easy, for example, to find out exact bank account balances. Some amounts you'll need to telephone outside sources for help. You could call a real estate agent in your area for an appraisal of the resale value of your home in today's market. Even simpler, check the newspaper real estate section for homes similar to yours in similar neighborhoods. How much are people asking for them?

For the value of your investments, you can check the values in the *Wall Street Journal* or call your financial advisor, lawyer, or whoever you have handling such matters. Other numbers will be your best estimate of whatever you think you could get for the item if you had to sell. Perhaps you own an antique Shirley Temple doll or an original Norman Rockwell painting. Try calling regional museums, curators, appraisers, antique shops. Read the classified sections. If you have a large collection of a certain item, it's probably worth checking one of the many publications that include price guides.

Most of us, however, have standard assets. After you've written as many of them down as you can, the next step is to organize them into categories.

The Quick and the Slow

Group together assets that could be most quickly converted into cash—within a few weeks at most. These *liquid* assets would include money in the bank, mutual funds, stocks, bonds, securities, partnerships, life insurance, gold, jewelry, silver, cars. Your goal is to have this set of assets add up to enough money to tide you over in the event of an illness, layoff, or some other change in your situation.

Write down in a separate list those assets that you *could* sell (liquidate) but that would be difficult to sell immediately because of complexity of investment, market timing, or some other restriction. Also on this list would be assets that would cause major tax penalties if you cashed them in prematurely. Retirement accounts, vested pensions, certificates of deposit (CDs), houses, stamps, coins, restricted stock, and limited partnerships all fall into this category.

Now you have a good, clean list of everything you own as well as a general idea of how easy it would be to get your hands on cash in an emergency. Are your assets balanced well between easy to sell or liquidate and slow to sell or restrictive? Do you have more than you thought? Have your assets increased or decreased in value? Are there items on your list you think aren't worth hanging on to anymore? Could you sell some things and use the cash to make better investments? Take a little time to ponder such questions before you begin working on the liabilities half of your net worth statement.

The Moment of Reckoning

What you owe, your liabilities, is probably easier to figure out than your assets but harder to accept. But you can't know your net worth unless you subtract your liabilities from your assets. On a new sheet of paper or page of your notebook, write down all outstanding bills, including rent, electricity, gas, water, telephone, cable TV, newspaper, insurance, grocery, and so on. Add credit card balances, mortgages, student loans, any other loans, personal debts, and income and property taxes.

In a separate column, write down the total dollar amounts of each item you owe money on. Include interest and finance charges on any applicable items such as credit cards, car loans, mortgages, and student loans. Sometimes these are "hidden" charges, so be extra careful looking for all your payments.

Now add up your total liabilities. Subtract this figure from your total assets and you have your net worth. If your liabilities are greater than your assets, your net worth is negative. If that's your situation, you're definitely reading the right book.

In any case, you've got your bottom line. You can update your net worth statement regularly to see where you've been and where you're going.

Appendix A (pages 208–211) contains two Net Worth Statement worksheets. One is simple, the other is a bit more detailed. Choose whichever one you think best suits your financial picture. Or make up your own, based on the information from this chapter. The important thing is to get an idea of your net worth sooner rather than later.

One More Asset You Might Have Missed

You may have noticed there is no space for Social Security on either of these worksheets. That's because it's a subject that many people find perplexing and that others are worried won't exist by the time they retire. We believe Social Security will continue to be part of every American's retirement income. True, there have been some changes in Social Security rules, but once you understand them, it will be easier to plug Social Security benefits into your retirement plans. And although the *percentage* of your retirement income from Social Security may be less than your parents' was, it would be a big mistake to discount it entirely. Margaret sums up our attitude: "We're not banking our future on Social Security. We understand it's supposed to be a supplement, not the backbone of our retirement funds."

What Is Social Security?

Until you start thinking seriously about retirement, Social Security may seem like nothing but a familiar nine-digit number. Or the amount in the box marked "deductions" on your paycheck stub. For as long as you work, you and your employer pay a percentage of your salary into the Social Security fund. Keep in mind this is *your* money, not the government's. It's just like other retirement or pension plans, except that it's not protected by the same sort of legislation.

The fund is divided into three parts: retirement, disability, and health insurance.

- Old age and survivors' insurance is to help support people when they are too old to work.
- Disability insurance is to help support those who become too ill or disabled to work.
- Health insurance, also known as Medicare, pays most of the hospital costs for those over retirement age. It also covers 80 percent of Medicare-approved doctors' fees.

If you make up to $61,200, by law you must pay 7.65 percent of your earnings to Social Security. For a single dental assistant who makes an annual salary of $26,244, each monthly paycheck would have the following deductions:

Gross Pay: $2,187.00
 Social Security Tax $135.59
 Medicare Tax $31.71

There would be other federal, state, and local deductions, but they'd vary. Notice that the Social Security and Medicare taxes add up to $167.30, which is 7.65 percent of this person's income.

If you make more than $61,200, you pay 6.2 percent of $61,200 into Social Security and 1.45 percent of whatever your *total* earnings are into Medicare. In other words, there is no limit for your Medicare contribution. Let's say you're a sharp sales rep who makes $71,200 a year in commissions. You'd pay 7.65

percent of $61,200, or $4,681.80, into Social Security/Medicare, *and* contribute 1.45 percent (or $145) of the $10,000 over the $61,200 you made.

The good news is that your employer matches the 7.65 percent you contribute. In reality, 15 percent of your income is invested in your Social Security account. The bad news is that if you're self-employed, you are your own employer, so you pay double. Don't worry about remembering to pay your own Social Security. The Internal Revenue Service kindly provides a form for you to include with your annual income tax return. Schedule SE is for self-employed people to figure their income tax, Social Security, and Medicare. If you happen to be a minister or a farmer, there will be special allowances. We know ministers and farmers aren't really self-employed—they're doing God's work.

> *Even with a pension and Social Security, people retiring in the future will not have enough. Everyone will need to invest.*
>
> —**Shirley Gross**

Who Qualifies

Anyone who has worked in this country for a minimum of 40 quarters (one quarter equals three months) qualifies for at least a portion of Social Security benefits. The 40 quarters do not have to be consecutive. For example, take a woman who works for three years and accumulates 12 quarters. She stays at home to raise children for 10 years and receives no credit toward Social Security. Then she goes back to work. Within seven years, she'd have her full 40 quarters and be eligible for Social Security benefits.

Social Security benefits are based on the 35 years you earned the most money. Say the woman above works from age 22 straight through to 65. But while her children are young, she works part time. The 35 highest-income years out of her 44 working years will count in calculating her Social Security benefits. That's good if you happen to be a late bloomer.

There is one other category of people that qualifies for Social Security. If you do not work but are married to a person who works, you will receive half the working spouse's benefit amount upon your spouse's retirement. That means your spouse receives his or her full benefit and, on top of that, you get a benefit. So a woman who works as a nurse all her life while her husband paints still lifes will collect about $900 a month when she retires at age 65. Her artist husband will be entitled to $450 a month.

If your spouse dies, you also are eligible for benefits based on the amount already paid in. If our hardworking nurse were to die, her husband would receive 100 percent, or $900 a month, in benefits.

What Will Your Benefit Be?

The easiest way to estimate your retirement benefits is to use the toll-free number the Social Security Administration provides. Although it's available Monday through Friday, from 7:00 A.M. to 7:00 P.M., you'll get through faster very early or very late. Dial 1-800-772-1213. If you have a touch-tone phone, you'll be told to press nine. Then you'll be given a choice of options. Choose the option called "Request for Statement of Earnings" card. You'll be prompted to spell out your name, street address, city, state, and zip code. The request form will be mailed to you within two weeks.

Once you return your request form, your "Perennial Earnings and Benefit Estimate Statement" will be sent back to you within six weeks. It takes about five minutes to fill out and asks for the following information:

1. Your name
2. Your Social Security number
3. Any other Social Security numbers you've ever used
4. Last year's actual earnings
5. This year's estimated earnings
6. The age you expect to retire
7. The average annual income you estimate you'll earn until then

After you receive your earnings and benefit statement, carefully check to see whether the amounts you've paid into Social Security over your lifetime seem in the right ballpark. It's good practice to file requests more than once. Some experts suggest every three years. That way you can check to see whether the records are accurate, keep tabs on how benefits will vary depending on what age you say you're going to retire, and make sure you've earned the 40-quarter credit. If you do spot any mistakes, you may have them corrected.

Naturally, if you prefer doing business in person, you can go to the closest Social Security office instead of using the telephone. Out of 1,300 offices around the country, there's bound to be one fairly close to you. Just look under "U.S. Government" in the telephone book for the Social Security address. If you have any question about the statement you receive, it's wise to straighten it out now, not wait until your retirement. Go to your local Social Security office and bring W-2 tax report forms or pay stubs with you to show how you think the government is in error.

Meanwhile, if you can't wait two months to get some idea of how much your benefits might be, you can look at Table 3.1. It will give you a very rough estimate.

Table 3.1: Social Security Monthly Benefits Estimate

Find the age closest to how old you are now in the first column. Go over to where that line intersects with how much you make now each year (your current annual salary). That number is approximately how much you can expect to receive from Social Security each month after you retire. (These figures are for unmarried workers. If you are married, the amount would be slightly higher.)

	CURRENT ANNUAL SALARY			
Your Current Age	$30,000	$40,000	$50,000	$55,000 and over
45 years	1,159	1,302	1,436	1,491
55 years	1,052	1,150	1,231	1,258
65 years	977	1,038	1,081	1,088

When You Can Collect

Social Security benefits vary according to your age at retirement. The government picks an age it calls "full retirement age." "Full" refers to the age you receive full, or 100 percent, of your benefits. Right now, the full retirement age is 65. If you retire before the designated age, you receive a prorated percentage of your benefits. If you retire at age 62, for example, you'd get 80 percent of your benefits.

Sounds simple so far, right? It would be except for the fact that the designated full retirement age is going to change gradually over the next several years. You will need to work two years longer—through age 67—to receive full benefits if you were born after 1959. For everyone born before 1938, the age remains 65. And for those born between 1938 and 1959, there is a sliding age range. Table 3.2 will help you determine at what age you'll qualify for full retirement benefits.

Table 3.2: Social Security Benefits Schedule by Age and Year of Birth

Find the year you were born. Under the years and months is the age you will be eligible for full retirement benefits.

**NORMAL RETIREMENT AGE FOR
FULL BENEFITS**

Year of Birth	Years	Months
1937 or before	65	0
1938	65	2
1939	65	4
1940	65	6
1941	65	8
1942	65	10
1943–1954	66	0
1955	66	2
1956	66	4
1957	66	6
1958	66	8
1959	66	10
1960 or later	67	0

That's assuming, of course, that you definitely want to wait until you qualify for 100 percent of your benefits. But there are a couple of alternatives.

1. You can retire at 62, taking a payment that would be smaller at first but gradually would go up with cost-of-living adjustments.
2. Wait until you're 70 to receive the largest possible payments.

There are pros and cons to both options, and financial advisors don't always agree on the best solution. When making the retirement age decision, consider:

- your health
- your expected life span
- your marital status
- how much you enjoy your job

Besides retirement, there are two other situations that qualify you for Social Security: widowhood or divorce. When your spouse dies, you collect 100 percent of whatever benefits he or she would get. A person who is married for 10 years or more can collect on an ex-husband or ex-wife's benefits after a divorce, even if the ex has remarried and even if the ex hasn't retired yet.

Hidden Assets

If you are discouraged about your net worth, take another pass at it. But this time around, keep in mind your hidden assets. These are assets that might be hard to assign a dollar value to at the moment but that do add to your net worth. Take out another sheet of paper to write down these "priceless" assets. For instance, have you considered your brain an asset? The more education and training you have, the greater your earning potential. A skilled worker will have greater assets than an unskilled worker. Yet no net worth statement we've ever seen has a space for "Ph.D."

The field you're in also becomes part of your net worth in a subtle way, depending on what's happening in the rest of society. During the baby boom, teachers were in great demand; during the Cold War, aerospace workers could name their jobs. Nowadays, fields such as computer programming and home health care are thriving. Buffy is grateful to her father for pointing her in a good direction, professionally speaking.

"My dad sent me to real estate school," Buffy says. "He realized what an expense it was to pay interest on inventory. He loved the idea that in real estate you pay nothing for your inventory: Your inventory is other people's homes. You owe these people your best efforts to sell their homes. But it doesn't cost you anything in terms of dollars."

Carol, too, has firsthand experience in the value of a good education. "Ways of doing things can change from generation to generation," she explains. "The older people did not buy anything unless they could pay cash for it. But education is an investment. By the time I realized I would have liked to have gone to college, the option was no longer there. Sometimes I wonder how it would have changed my life. I had worked at a local air-conditioning manufacturer for 22 years as a secretary and in personnel, shipping, and accounting. When the company closed I was classified as a 'dis-

> *We helped send our two children to college through regular savings accounts. We set up accounts for them early on and made monthly deposits, and more at their birthdays and holidays. They each had a weekly* **TV Guide** *route and were allowed to keep some of the money they earned, but most of it went into their accounts. When their paternal grandmother passed away, they each got a small inheritance, which they used for school. In addition to their accounts, they worked during the summers and school terms, and they received financial aid and loans which, I'm pleased to say, they've paid back. None of this seems to me like what you'd call "advanced financial thinking." It's common sense, and it's worked for us.*
>
> *—Ann Brewer*

placed worker,' and that made our son eligible for some special student loans. We felt it was important for him to participate in financing his education. College is expensive on parents, and kids need to know it's not all served up on a silver platter. I think savings and education both fall under the banner of 'Preparing for the Future.' "

Another hidden asset might be your family. If you have a wealthy older relative, you might inherit some of that wealth eventually. Maybe the thought makes you feel uncomfortable, but you might as well consider the possibility. The fact is that if you stand to benefit from the natural passing on of resources from one generation to the next, your asset position is different from that of someone with no relatives.

The same idea applies to your grown children. While taking money from your own children may go against the grain in this country, it's quite acceptable and even expected in most other cultures. If you're fortunate enough to have highly successful kids—thanks to parents who put them through college—there's a good chance they'll be able to help you in return, especially as their income levels rise while yours lowers during retirement.

Hazel has had some help from relatives, for which she's most grateful. "Before my husband died," says Hazel, "I promised him I would help take care of his sisters, both of whom were maiden ladies. I made many two-week trips back to Chicago to look after them in their later years. After they died, my brother-in-law Bob

set up a retirement fund, which sent me a monthly check. Recently my nephew established another mutual fund for me. I took care of those women for many years, and here they were taking care of me. It wasn't something I expected and eventually it did run out, but it was a great help."

After you've worked your way through this chapter, you should have a solid picture of your finances. The next step is to paint the picture brighter by teaching yourself how to save enough to invest in your future.

Finishing Stitch

1. FIGURE OUT HOW MUCH YOU OWN.

2. FIGURE OUT HOW MUCH YOU OWE.

3. DON'T DISCOUNT SOCIAL SECURITY.

4. DID WE MENTION THE IMPORTANCE OF SAVING?

CHAPTER FOUR

Cut the Coat According to the Cloth

RUNNING STITCH:

Pay Yourself First

We all know people who are natural-born savers. Beardstown has its share of them. There must be something in the water here that encourages saving, because some of us even remember saving during the hardest times. "It was the Depression when I came out of high school," Helen Kramer says, "and I was fortunate to get a job at First State Bank in Beardstown. In 1934 I was making $40 a month. Even then I was trying to put a little away regularly in a passbook savings account, but it was difficult for many years because of low salaries. In the 1960s I tried to put away $100 per month. That was a quarter of what I was earning then."

"I've always been a saver," says Ruth. "I save everything. I grew up on a farm and we raised calves, sold them, and saved the money. When I was in high school I found a way to bank a dollar every Monday."

Like Helen and Ruth, a lot of us have the best intentions in the world when it comes to saving money. We work hard, make good salaries, and surely don't squander our money. Yet by the time we've paid our bills, bought some food, and maybe gone to a movie, there's nothing left to save. We vow that next month will be different. Next month we'll cut back spending somewhere so we can start saving for our retirement. Or the kids' college tuition. Or maybe even just our summer vacation.

Next month comes. Next month goes. Still no money left over to save. Where is that money going? Maybe we think that if we just make a little bit more each year, we'll have no problem saving. Think about this for a minute: Aren't you making more money now than when you first started out? Yet didn't you used to have enough for a trip home or Christmas presents for the family? Now that you're making more, do you save any more? Are you putting away thousands of dollars a year toward your retirement? If you're like more than half of Americans, the answer is no. But why not?

Until we have a good understanding of where our money is going, it's hard to manage it well. And if we can't manage it, we can't save it. If we can't save it, we can't invest it. And if we can't invest it, we can't make it grow into a comfortable nest egg.

This chapter will help you look at the relationship between

your paycheck and your spending patterns. Then it will discuss the single most important habit in the whole book. This habit is the way to building a nest egg: Pay yourself first.

"More than any of us, Lillian was a champion of the idea 'Pay yourself first,'" Maxine recalls. "She'd always tell me, 'Save first, then pay your bills.'"

When people think of managing money, they often think it means an old-fashioned budget. But a budget is one part of finances, together with a financial plan, net worth statement, and investment portfolio. A net worth statement is like a still photograph of your finances. A budget is like a moving picture, an action plan for reaching your financial goals. It's not an end in itself; it's a means to growing your nest egg and enjoying yourself. The goals you wrote down in Chapter 1—along with a clear sense of your net worth from Chapter 3—can now help you focus on your day-to-day spending and savings plan. You need to know how much you're spending, what you're spending it on, and where you can cut back spending. That's the key amount you'll then have to invest and increase your assets by taking advantage of compound interest.

"I really try to hammer home to my clients that they should be saving 20 percent of their gross income," says one financial planner. If you're spending more than you're making, you could probably spend less. If you're spending more than you're making *and* you're not saving any money, you could probably spend much less. If you're making more than you're spending but you're not paying yourself the difference—through investments—you're actually losing your own money.

Like many of the Beardstown Ladies, Doris Edwards relates finances to farming. "Growing up on a farm we raised our own pork, beef, and poultry," she says. "We had a big garden and an apple orchard, and we canned our own fruit and vegetables. We stored it in the cellar for winter. We knew we couldn't eat what we didn't have.

"I think this applies to money, too. This rule has always worked for me: If you can't afford it, don't buy it and then you don't have to worry about it."

Sort It Out

The first step is to sort out your spending so you can better analyze it. This doesn't have to be a very detailed process. You're just trying to get a rough idea of categories in which you spend money. List the six largest areas. For most people these are:

1. Rent or mortgage (include property taxes and utilities here)
2. Food
3. Medical expenses (include dentist, prescriptions, doctor visits, insurance premiums)
4. Car (include gas, insurance, tune-ups, and payments)
5. Entertainment (include movies, restaurants, parties, gifts)
6. Home items (include furniture, electronic equipment, home repairs, landscaping costs)
7. Everything else (This is that category that seems to have a mind of its own. It's where you list clothes, haircuts, impulse items, loans to your brother-in-law, the kids' allowances, raffle tickets . . . It's the first place to look in your budget when you want to find money to save.)

To see how your spending compares to how much you have to spend, add up three months' worth of your family's total wages, after withholding taxes. Divide by three. You have your average monthly income.

Now take out your checkbook, credit card statements, and any cash withdrawals slips or receipts from banks or automatic teller machines. As you go through your records, put each check amount or credit card charge in the category that it fits most closely. Add up the total amounts for three months. Divide that number by three. You now have your average monthly spending.

You need to write down a target figure for each category of spending. Then each month add up what you *actually* spent in each category. If your actual expenses are much greater than your target goal, you can try to adjust either the target or the spending. The key is to be as specific as possible. Instead of just having a category for medical expenses, you might try subcategories such as office visits, prescriptions, dentist, and eyeglasses. Or grocery bills, takeout food, restaurants, and wine and beer.

You can try shifting from one category to another or cutting way back the next

month. For example, maybe you went overboard on entertaining and gifts in the month of June, what with all those graduations, wedding showers, and company picnics. You spent about $200 more than you had planned for. What do you do?

You could get upset with yourself. Or you could forget about it. Wouldn't it be better to accept that every June these occasions come up and every June you need to budget $200 extra? That way you can save somewhere else—maybe you don't need a new outfit every spring—and enjoy June again.

"Once you get on the budget bandwagon," Carol points out, "things have a way of building. Just the other day Bill said, 'I'd rather buy a little bit cheaper car and put some money away in stocks.' That's not something I would have heard from him before."

Finding the Leaks, Plugging the Holes

The next step is to find out in more detail where your money is leaking out of your budget. You probably have a big amount of cash you spent but just can't account for. Where did it go? Some people say it seems to go up in smoke, or fly out the window. Even if you write it down under Miscellaneous, it's gone forever—unless you track it like a bloodhound. There are several ways to keep track of your spending, depending on your accounting style.

The most accurate, most often advised system is to write down every single cent that you spend for at least a week. It's better if you can do it for a month, and the better still if you can manage three months. Although this is really hard to do, once you've accomplished the exercise you probably won't have to do it again. It's amazing how effective writing down your expenses can be in making you aware of how money can disappear into little nothings, quarter by quarter.

Maybe you buy a cup of coffee every morning on your way to work. It costs 75 cents. Big deal, you say. But if you start writing it down and adding it up, you soon see that your coffee habit is costing you almost $200 a year. Two hundred dollars is harder to write off than 75 cents, isn't it?

Ten Steps to a Budget

Follow these steps for your best budget.

1. Write down all your fixed monthly expenses by category (mortgage, taxes, insurance, car payments).
2. Divide fixed bills that you pay once or twice a year into monthly amounts. (Example: If your homeowner's insurance is $400 a year, you'd include $35 in your monthly budget statement.)
3. Estimate all variable monthly expenses by averaging last year's total expenses by category (food, clothes, entertainment, vacation, utilities, home maintenance, car maintenance, medical).
4. Add up all expenses and write TOTAL.
5. Add up all after-tax income and write TOTAL. Don't include occasional extra income such as overtime, royalties, or dividends. If you are paid weekly, multiply by 4.3 for a monthly budget. If you are paid every two weeks, check to see whether that month you are getting two or three paychecks.
6. Make a deposit in an account just for savings. Either

mail a check to an investment account or have an automatic deduction made into an account.

7. Pay other necessary bills.

8. Compare how your spending and planning compare each month.

9. Discuss any major purchases or upcoming expenses. Decide on a strategy for paying them without reducing your savings plan.

10. Congratulate yourself for having a budget, whether you meet your financial goal or not. At least you're taking charge of your financial life.

There are lots of different kinds of budget forms. Usually finding one you like and can use takes some trial and error. The type we have found helpful is a notebook with preprinted accounting pages. These are called "Household Budget" books and can be found in stationery and office supply stores for a few dollars. You can fill in your own categories month to month. As your family grows and changes, you can easily change the categories in your budget book to suit your circumstances. Use a budget book, try the forms in Appendix A, or make up your own.

Another system is to pay important bills, such as mortgage and utilities, first. Then list what you *must* buy that month (food, medicine). Any amount beyond that put into savings—before you can spend it. Sylvia Gaushell and her husband put some money into savings every month. The amount varied depending on the bills they had. Sylvia says, "I understand that people nowadays have problems with saving. You can't save it if you haven't got it. But I think it helps to have somewhere to put the money. Once you've started a savings account or a program, it becomes like your most important bill and you find a way to pay it."

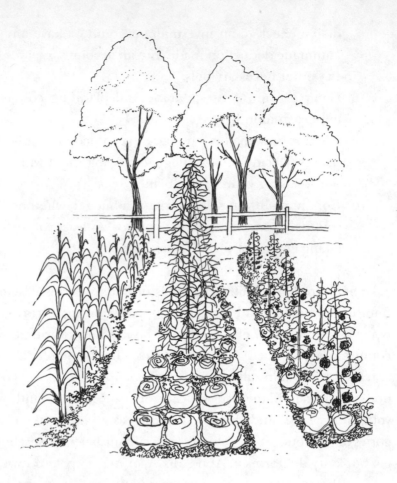

Stop and Consider

Hazel's whole attitude toward life is what helps her save money. "I attribute a good bit to the fact that I don't want a lot," she says. "I go shopping with someone and she comes home with an arm-load of knickknacks. I come home with nothing. But I've had just as good a time. I've always been fortunate that if I can't afford something, I don't really want it."

With Hazel in mind, think about what you *need* as opposed to what you *want*. Go through your budget with a fine-toothed comb. Are there areas you could cut back somehow? First, take a look at your biggest budget categories, your fixed expenses. Could you refinance your mortgage at a lower interest rate? Do you need life insurance on your children? If you switched your auto insurance company to your homeowner's insurance company, would you get a discount? Maybe you could get along fine with one car instead of two. Maybe now that your kids are grown, you don't need as much property. The point is to keep an open mind and look for as many ways as possible to reduce your current necessary spending so that you can increase your future retirement spending.

No matter what your situation, you can save money. If you see that you are spending more than you want to, consider these painless, easy ways to save money. Some of them will work for you and others won't, but by adopting one of these habits today, you'll be better off tomorrow. (Don't worry, we're not going to suggest saving string or reusing old coffee filters.)

The Beardstown Ladies' Best Budget Tips

- Try house brands or generic brands of paper goods and other basics.
- Think about how to get the most out of the entertainment you spend your hard-earned money on. Did you have fun the last time you went to the movies, which added up to $30 after paying the sitter, the tickets, the parking, and the popcorn? Is it worth the price of admission, or would it be better to rent a video? Or would you have even more fun if you spent almost nothing and played Pictionary with friends?

- Speaking of videos, do check out your public libraries. In our opinion, libraries are the greatest. Why buy videos, CDs, books on tape, magazines, or novels when you can borrow them for free?
- Take advantage of free entertainment whenever you can.
- Consider your mode of transportation. Would it be cheaper to ride a bike? Car pool? Buy a smaller car? Or even walk?
- Repair machines rather than buying new ones right away.
- Break the credit card habit. If you can't cut up those cards, put yourself on a credit diet. As Hazel says, "Those credit cards are ruining people."
- When you're about to buy something brand new, ask yourself, "Do I really need this?"
- Each time you give up a costly habit or finish paying off a loan, continue depositing that amount into a savings or investment account.
- Bag it. Bring lunch to work, send lunch to school. If you can't make it every day, aim for at least a few days a week.
- Some people never buy anything at full price—on principle. Shop for sales.
- Instead of buying expensive gifts, could you offer a service? Lots of times, these kinds of gifts are more meaningful than anything material. A young family might love a gift of baby-sitting; an older friend would surely appreciate an outing; a busy two-career couple could use a reliable dog walker.
- Think about how you spend your leisure time. Does it cost a lot? Could you take up jogging instead of golf?

Would your local YMCA have weight-lifting equipment as good as an expensive health club?

- The catalogs that stuff your mailbox entice you to buy, buy, buy. Recycle them right away and you'll be less likely to order something you don't really need.
- Shop with a list and stick with it—unless you see a true bargain on a product your family uses regularly. Then it's often more economical to stock up.
- Never go to the grocery store on an empty stomach.
- Use those coupons.
- Watch for double coupon days. Savings really add up.

Some of us think saving money is one of the most creative, fun things we do. Try turning it into a game the whole family can play and come up with your own ideas.

Pay Yourself First

This one simple idea can work financial wonders for people who don't want to be bothered with a budget. These people say having to count every penny or plan every expense takes the fun out of life. If you're like that, fine. Just pay yourself first. It's a tested, workable solution.

- Every month or every two weeks, whatever schedule you get paid on, you present yourself with a bill for savings.
- Use a preaddressed envelope, a notation in your checkbook, or an automatic deduction from your bank account.

- Make a deposit in some kind of savings plan before you write a single check, pay a single bill, take out a single dollar.
- You can start as low as 1 or 2 percent of your income. It's better to begin with a tiny amount than to put off ever beginning because you think it's not enough. Ann Brewer says she and her husband put money away in savings every month—"sometimes not a lot. You could say, savings has been a part of the fabric of our lives."
- Eventually you can make it 10 percent or 15 percent. Some financial planners even suggest 20 percent. But first just get started.
- It's important to get into the habit and not let a paycheck go by without paying yourself.

The great part of paying yourself first is that it puts you on an automatic budget. As long as you're paying all the necessary bills, you'll know without having to do much math how much extra you have left to spend. You won't even need to make up a budget for every month. Your miscellaneous cash expenditures will decrease out of necessity. And you'll know that month in and month out, you're paying yourself and investing in your own future.

One of the very best ways to pay yourself first is through automatic payroll deductions. Carol is a big believer in payroll deductions. She says, "I work at DeSollar Insurance, a family insurance company in Beardstown. I'm licensed to sell personal lines such as life, health, home, and auto. I've purchased an annuity through one of the major insurance companies we work with, and the payments are taken directly from each paycheck. I don't see the money and I don't miss the money. It goes to the annuity and it just keeps growing."

Finishing Stitch

1. ANALYZE WHERE YOUR MONEY GOES.

2. ADJUST YOUR SPENDING, IF NECESSARY.

3. PAY YOURSELF FIRST. (THIS IS ANOTHER WAY OF SAYING SAVE.)

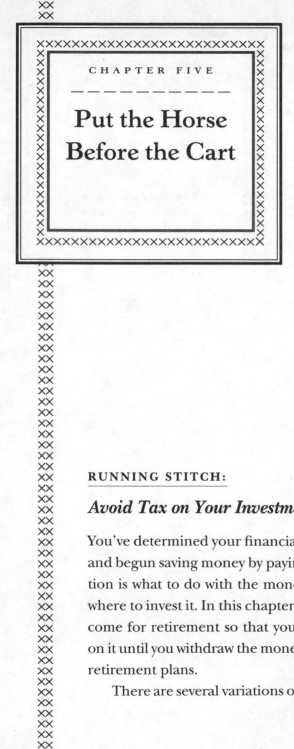

CHAPTER FIVE

Put the Horse Before the Cart

RUNNING STITCH:

Avoid Tax on Your Investment

You've determined your financial goals, figured your net worth, and begun saving money by paying yourself first. The next question is what to do with the money you have to invest: how and where to invest it. In this chapter we'll describe ways to invest income for retirement so that you don't have to pay income tax on it until you withdraw the money. These are called tax-deferred retirement plans.

There are several variations on the tax-deferred theme. We'll describe the pros and cons of 401(k)s, Keoghs, SEPs, and IRAs. But first it's helpful to understand *why* investigating and using at least one of these plans is crucial to your financial future.

It used to be you would work for one company for 40 years, retire, and receive a pension. But traditional pensions have been getting scarcer. There's been a trend among corporations and small companies across the country to put more responsibility back onto the employee to provide for retirement. As Shirley states, "I have no pension and my Social Security is small, so I have counted on my investments to enable me to live comfortably in my retirement."

Also, more workers move from job to job, company to company. Even if you work for a company that does provide a pension, chances are good that you'll forfeit most of it by quitting—or, in the worst-case situation, by being laid off—before it's fully vested. Ann Brewer's husband worked for a local air-conditioning manufacturer for 26 years until it closed in 1989. He retired as a supervisor and would have received full pension if he could have stayed until 65. Instead he received a reduced company pension.

The problem is that companies didn't really want to advertise the fact that pensions were getting hard to come by. So a lot of baby boomers have been caught without any plans. That's why there is a bigger need than ever before for "mobile" pensions: pensions that you set up, you contribute to, and you can take with you from company to company during your whole working life.

An advantage to this system is that you have more freedom to invest your retirement money in the way you think is best. Carol's been thinking about this opportunity a lot lately. She says, "For years I've known that my retirement money from my previous job is out there in some large money fund. I'm getting the confidence to find out exactly where it is and see about investing it myself. Even if there is a penalty for taking it before retirement age, I might be better off managing it myself."

Different Plans Are Good for Different Folks

We think once you see these examples, they'll seem like offers you can't refuse. Listen to Buffy on the subject: "IRAs and Keoghs are wonderful instruments. All the money you deposit in them each year can be subtracted from your adjusted gross income at tax time. For every $1,000 you deposit, the government, in effect, kicks in a few hundred dollars—the amount you would have had to pay in taxes on that money.

"You don't have to pay taxes until you withdraw the money, which you can't do without penalty until you are 59 1/2. But by that time I figure I'll be slowing down and in a lower tax bracket, so I'll not only have the interest earned, but I will have succeeded in paying lower taxes on that money. What this says to me is there is no free lunch, but there is a subsidized lunch. All the rest is gravy."

If Buffy doesn't whet your appetite for an IRA, take a look at the following comparison of investments, one taxable and the other tax-deferred. It assumes an investor in the 28 percent tax bracket invests $2,000 each year in a vehicle with a 10 percent return.

	Taxable Investment	Tax-deferred IRA
After 20 years	$84,272	$126,005
After 30 years	$189,588	$361,887

After 20 years, the tax-deferred investment is worth $126,005. The ordinary investment, which has been taxed each year for those 20 years, is worth $84,272.

Next we have a comparison between a 401(k) plan investment and an ordinary investment, again after 20 years. The 401(k) money is not only tax-deferred, it's tax-deductible each year.

	Ordinary Investment	401(k) Investment
Annual contribution	$2,000	$2,000
28% income tax	560	0
Actual amount to invest	1,440	2,000
Total investment	40,000	40,000
Value if earning 8% after 20 years, assuming ordinary investment income taxed every year at 28%	$57,625	91,524

Of course, everyone's situation is different. You will want to check with an accountant, financial planner, or employee benefits representative before deciding which plan is right for you. "So many companies are offering menu-type benefits where employees can pick and choose what they want," Betty reminds us. "This is where I would encourage people to take advantage of whatever they can. Don't let it slide just to get that extra dollar or two in your paycheck each month."

401(k)s: A Really Good Deal

The 401(k) plan, named after a section of the Internal Revenue Service code, is one of the very best deals around. These plans are popular for good reason. The benefits of 401(k) plans include:

1. They provide retirement funds.
2. You get to contribute part of your income *before it's taxed.*
3. The money is invested to accrue interest, which is *tax-deferred.*
4. Your 401(k) contribution is deducted from your paycheck automatically.
5. It is yet another way to pay yourself first.

The plans let employees have part of their salary set aside in a special fund earmarked for them and not taxed until it's withdrawn at retirement time. You decide how much you want to put into your 401(k) and where you want the money invested, and it's deducted from your paycheck automatically. (If you work in government or certain tax-exempt organizations, the plan will be called a 403[b].) As we saw in Chapter 3, this is another way of paying yourself first. Carol explains why 401(k)s have been so effective for her family.

"Bill works for CIPS, the local gas and electric utility, and he has his 401(k) money deducted from his paycheck," she says. "If we didn't do it this way, the money would come into our house, it would get eaten up by bills, and we would never see it again. It's our way of paying ourselves first."

Another great feature is that most companies add to or even match your contribution. Now think about that for a minute.

You're saving for your retirement without having to lift a finger, you're reducing your current income tax, and you're getting extra—free—money from your employer. It's almost too good to be true. Betty is proof that it really works. She has a 401(k) through the bank where she works. The bank matches what she contributes up to a maximum of 6 percent. "I take full advantage of it," Betty says, "with 6 percent of my salary going straight from my paycheck into that plan."

A lot of people say they can't afford to live on less than their full take-home pay. But really, they can't afford not to have money deducted for a 401(k) plan. Why? Because of the tax situation, you end up with *more* total investment if you participate in a 401(k). Take a look at the following case.

If You're Single and Have No Dependents	Without a 401(k)	With a 401(k)
Salary	$25,000	$25,000
You contribute 10%	0	2,500
Net salary	$25,000	$22,500
Federal withholding tax	2,790	2,415
Social Security and Medicare tax	1,912	1,912
Take-home pay	20,298	18,173
Amount invested and earning 8%	0	2,500
The bottom line (the amount you keep)	**$20,298**	**$20,673**

But wait, that's not all. After 40 years, if you keep the money in the 401(k) plan earning 8 percent, you'll have $54,311 without investing any more during all those years.

You need to keep in mind that 401(k) plans are definitely for retirement savings only. To remind people, the government says you can't touch the money until you're 59 1/2. If you do withdraw it before then, you'll be taxed on it like regular income, plus you'll be charged an extra 10 percent of the total as a penalty.

On the other hand, if you find yourself needing cash for college tuition or some other reason, you can borrow up to 50 percent, or $50,000, of your vested 401(k) balance. You pay back the interest on this loan to yourself, so it's a way to obtain inexpensive financing that IRAs and SEPs don't offer.

You can't put your whole salary into a 401(k), but you can put more than into some other retirement funds: 15 percent of your salary, up to a limit that changes each year to keep pace with inflation. For 1995, that limit was $9,240.

The mobile part of the 401(k) pension comes into play when you switch from Company A to Company B. You get to take every dollar you contributed yourself and any income it has earned. How much of your employer's contribution you get to take with you depends on how long you've worked there. You

can then either put it into the new company's retirement plan or roll it over into an Individual Retirement Account. Which brings us to . . .

The Ins and Outs of Individual Retirement Accounts

Individual Retirement Accounts (IRAs) were an instant success after the government first introduced them in 1981 to encourage Americans to save more. Anyone who earned a living could contribute 10 percent of his or her income—up to $2,000—into a special account through a bank, brokerage, or mutual fund. Who wouldn't jump at the chance to deduct $2,000 a year right off the top of their income and not have it taxed? What if you could invest that $2,000 a year and not have the interest taxed, either? No wonder that, as soon as IRAs started, Helen put everything allowable into one at the end of each year.

IRAs had lots of advantages back then. Besides tax deferrals and tax deductions, IRAs let you be very flexible. You could contribute all $2,000 on April 14 and still deduct the contribution from your previous year's income. Or you could spread out your payments and add a little every month. You could even skip a year if you were feeling strapped for cash.

They were so appealing, in fact, that Americans flocked to them like ducks to bread crumbs. The federal government was worried that too much money was being tax-sheltered. So it decided to sharply reduce those tax benefits. Since 1986, deductions for IRA contributions have been limited to the following:

- Workers without other pension plans
- Married couples with less than $50,000 annual income
- Single people who earn less than $35,000

If you make more than the above amounts or if you or your spouse qualifies for any company pension plan, you can't deduct your IRA contribution from your taxable income. Does that mean you shouldn't have an IRA? Not necessarily. For starters, the tax laws keep changing. There's even been talk of getting rid of some of the penalties and taxes for withdrawing IRA money before you're the usual age of 59 1/2 under certain conditions. The point is that to take advantage of any retirement savings plan, you need to keep up on the changing rules.

An IRA is usually self-directed or custodial. If it's self-directed, you can choose whatever sort of investment you want for your IRA, from certificates of deposit to mutual funds, from individual stocks to bonds. If it's custodial, the bank where you buy your IRA keeps track of where it's invested. Even if the original contribution isn't deductible, your investment earnings still are protected from taxation as long as the money is kept in the IRA. Any tax on the interest earned is deferred until you withdraw from the IRA. That difference can be worthwhile if the IRA is kept for 20 or 30 years. All those years your taxes are postponed, your extra money is earning compound interest. No matter how you slice it, paying Uncle IRA is better than paying Uncle Sam. It's easy to see why if we look at two Beardstown Ladies.

Let's say Carol opens an IRA. She invests $2,000 in a mutual fund that yields 8 percent interest. She adds $1,000 each year for the next 10 years. She thus earns $19,684. Elsie invests $2,000 in the same mutual fund, but not through an IRA. Although she also adds $1,000 to it each year and also earns 8 percent interest, at the end of 10 years she has $11,802. That's $7,882 less than Carol, or the difference between a vacation in Tahiti and a trip to Lake Michigan. Why? Because the government is taking out a third of Elsie's investment in taxes. Instead of investing $2,000, she's really investing $1,400. And instead of earning 8 percent interest, her money is making 5.6 percent because the interest income is taxed, as well.

IRAs penalize you for early withdrawals: 10 percent, just like 401(k) plan penalties. One advantage they have over 401(k) plans is that you can invest IRAs in practically anything. With 401(k) plans, you're limited to whatever options the company offers.

Another fact worth considering about IRAs is the timing of your contribution. If you contribute $2,000 to your IRA on January 1 instead of April 15 each year, it will mean a $6,000 difference in 10 years and a $16,000 difference in 20 years—remember the power of compound interest and time? You might decide it's worth paying yourself sooner rather than later.

Annuities

Annuities come in all sorts of shapes and sizes, but they each offer tax-deferred income for the future. Usually sold by life insurance companies, annuities are like a policy you buy to provide yourself with income after you retire. You pay into an annuity while you're working, and then you're guaranteed a monthly income for a certain period of time or, more commonly, for the rest of your life. The way you pay into an annuity or the way you receive your annuity payments is what makes them so varied. Three main types are *immediate, deferred variable,* and *deferred fixed-rate* annuities.

When you retire, you might want to buy an immediate or single-premium annuity, as they are sometimes called, with money you receive from a pension plan. Then you are guaranteed income for your lifetime. The company figures out what that amount will be based on how much you pay in (usually there's a $5,000 minimum), interest rates, and life expectancy tables.

A deferred variable annuity is one in which your money is invested in a mutual fund, but any earnings are tax-deferred until after you retire and start receiving your annuity payments. The "variable" refers to the fact that how much your investment will be worth will depend on how your mutual fund has done. When you retire, you can choose whether you want to switch it to an immediate annuity and get paid or retrieve the money and reinvest it.

Deferred fixed-rate annuities mean you invest an amount in the beginning that is guaranteed a certain interest rate. After an agreed-on time period, a new interest rate may be set. In this way, fixed-rate annuities are similar to certificates of deposit.

There is no limit on how much you can contribute to an annuity, and the tax advantage is a definite plus. But keep in mind that the fees and early withdrawal penalties insurance companies may charge can really add up. So annuities are a better choice for those who are relatively young and can keep building a retirement nest egg for a long time.

What If You're Self-Employed?

At last count, 50 million Americans are self-employed. And Margaret's one of them. Since she and her husband work for themselves, neither of them is going to have a fat company pension. Margaret says, "That's why it's so important we make plans on our own. We've started IRAs, but only recently."

If you're self-employed you won't have a company pension or a company-sponsored 401(k) plan. But you can still save tax-deferred dollars for your retirement through several plans.

KEOGH PLANS

Keogh plans—named after U.S. Representative Eugene James Keogh, who helped introduce the idea—are especially for the self-employed. There are three different types of Keogh plans.

1. The *profit-sharing* Keogh. You decide every year how much or how little you want to contribute and deduct from your taxes, up to 13 percent of your income after deducting the contribution. The amount can be as little as zero but cannot be more than $30,000. This kind of Keogh is flexible and the most common.

2. The *money-purchase* Keogh lets you contribute as much as 20 percent of your income (after deducting the contribution) *if* you contribute the same percentage you initially choose every single year. If you can't cough up the money one year, you'll be charged a penalty. This kind of Keogh is best for the more affluent self-employed.

> *Sometimes people work both for a company and work for themselves. Then what category are they in? Let's say you work for Macy's as the head of a department. But you also design and sell a small line of dresses under your own name. You could participate in Macy's 401(k) plan. In addition, you could start a Keogh to shelter part of the money you make as a dress designer.*

3. The *combination* Keogh is just how it sounds: the best of both worlds. You have a money-purchase plan set at 10 percent. On top of that, you have a profit-sharing plan to take whatever you can afford beyond the 10 percent each year, up to a $30,000 maximum contribution.

To set up a Keogh, you first have to decide what type of investment you want to fund it. Then you go straight to that vehi-

Before you're ready to choose which baskets to put your eggs into or how to fund your IRA, SEP, or 401(k), you need to understand a few basic principles of investing. That's what our next chapter is all about: how to think about investing.

cle for a Keogh application form: banks for certificate of deposits, insurance companies for annuities, mutual fund companies for mutual funds. Keoghs require an annual tax return called Form 5500. If you hold a Keogh, you must be on the lookout for frequent changes in the federal regulations on retirement plans, too.

After you've completed the application form, return it to the same institution. For more information on setting up Keoghs and other related retirement plans, you can call the Internal Revenue Service at 1-800-829-3676 and ask for Publication 560, *Retirement Plans for the Self-Employed.*

SIMPLIFIED EMPLOYEE PENSION PLANS

If Keoghs seem like too much bother, then you're a good candidate for Simplified Employee Pension plans, or SEPs. These aren't as well known, although they've been in existence since 1978, but they are exceptional. SEPs are not only simple, they're more flexible because they're administered like IRAs, yet they allow tax-deductible contributions of much more than the $2,000 IRA limit—about 13 percent of your net income (up to $30,000 when combined with other plans).

SARSEP stands for Salary Reduction Simplified Employee Pension Plan. These are voluntary programs in which an employee voluntarily has a salary deduction. The difference is then put into a pension plan that can be invested. The employee winds up with less taxable income and a tax-sheltered retirement plan. According to one financial planner we talked with, small business owners like SEPS and SARSEPS because of their low administrative costs.

Finishing Stitch

1. REALIZE YOU NEED TO PRO-
   VIDE YOUR OWN PENSION.

2. TAKE ADVANTAGE OF RE-
   TIREMENT SAVINGS PLANS.

3. MAKE IT EASY ON YOURSELF
   TO SAVE.

CHAPTER SIX

Don't Put All Your Eggs in One Basket

RUNNING STITCH:

Diversify Your Investments to Limit Risk

By now you know that to grow a comfortable nest egg you need to think about your retirement, use the power of compound interest, figure your net worth, pay yourself first, and find tax-sheltered investment plans. The next step is to learn a few basic principles of investing. This chapter will teach you how to diversify, how to approach risk and reward, how to allocate your assets, and how to stick with an investment strategy through different stages of life.

Ruth Huston is a good example of a person who started out not knowing enough but who is now a model investor. How did she make the change? By educating herself.

When Ruth's husband died, she put his life insurance money into certificates of deposit. "This was still several years before I joined the investment club, and I didn't know any better," Ruth says. "Today I have a more balanced portfolio. I inherited some stocks, including shares in a local grain elevator and the local utility. The dividends on these stocks come in handy. I've also purchased some stocks for myself, primarily RPM, the stock I follow for the club. RPM is an Ohio-based manufacturer of protective coatings and paints. I loved it from the first time I heard it had 46 consecutive years of record earnings.

"At different times during my life I have also owned government bonds. I even bought some bonds for my son and my niece and nephews and put the bonds in their names."

Putting all her money into certificates of deposit meant her total investment was in one place. It was safe, but, at fairly low interest rates, it was barely keeping Ruth's savings even with inflation. Fortunately, Ruth learned how to diversify her investments. While that may sound like a fancy Wall Street term, it's not.

Diversifying your investments means putting your money in different financial instruments. Does that mean investing in 20 different bonds, partnerships, stocks, futures, options, real estate, and certificates of deposit? No, that would be time-consuming, confusing, and unnecessary. You can spread your risk by carefully choosing three to five investments. Doris explains, "I don't want all my eggs in one basket. I started an IRA and I've saved regularly at a savings and loan. I've also got some money in a mutual fund. I'm not a closet millionaire, but I think I've lived and saved sensibly."

Diversification is the best single investment strategy for generating the greatest return for the least risk. That's what this chapter will help you discover. In a perfect world, there would be such a thing as no-risk, high-reward investments. But take our word for it: There is no such thing. If it seems too good to be true, it usually *is* too good to be true. So while we may not live in a perfect world, if we are sensible about balancing our investments—not too risky, not too safe—we should receive ample reward yet still be able to sleep at night.

The Three Rs: Risk, Reward, Return

Thirty years ago a man bought his new granddaughter a $1,000 U.S. Savings Bond. The girl's grandmother bought her 100 shares of stock at $10 apiece in a small company that made typewriter ribbons.

The generous investments the baby's grandparents made for her seemed sensible at the time. But today that bond is worth very little because of the rate of inflation. And the typewriter company went under with the advent of personal computers. Her shares are worthless.

Both grandparents made the same investment mistake: They didn't spread the investment risk. Her grandfather played it too safe and didn't get enough return on investment. Her grandmother gambled too much and lost everything.

Investments can be looked at in several ways. For long-term financial planning, we need to know how much *return* or *reward* we can expect from each kind of investment. How much money might we get back? Then we need to know how much *risk* we must take in order to receive that reward. How much money might we lose? Maybe investing in soybean futures promises an amazing 20 percent return on your money—but at the risk of losing every dime if soybean prices plummet. That's what we'd call a high-risk, high-reward investment. At the other end of the spectrum is a savings account. You put your money in the bank, it earns a puny 2 percent interest, but you're in virtually no danger of ever losing it. That's the ultimate low-risk, low-reward investment.

The most common way investments are classified is from low risk to high risk. As the risk increases, the chances of greater return increase, too. Low-risk investments include savings accounts, money market funds (don't mix these up with mutual funds), and certificates of deposit. Next is the limited-risk category with blue-chip stocks, Treasury bonds, zero-coupon bonds, and corporate and municipal bonds. In the moderate-risk category we have stock mutual funds, growth stocks, and some kinds of real estate. Finally, for the daredevils, are the high-risk investments: futures, options, speculative stocks, commodities, and junk bonds. Figure 6.1 depicts the risk versus the reward of investments in the various risk categories.

Figuring out the "risk-reward" ratio of different types of investments is not something you have to do by yourself. Financial experts have been studying and analyzing this subject for years. You can pretty well trust the general guidelines they've come up with.

Carnell, referring to the major investment she made in her pork production farm, says, "We still have a large investment in the business and it's still considered high risk. Everything from the cost of feed to the price you get when you sell your hogs can change at a moment's notice. Some people might think, 'My goodness, you've gambled your way through life!' When we were borrowing heavily to make our business grow and experiencing major shifts in prices, we sometimes had nearly as much in loans as we had in equity. But farmers understand that as their busi-

FIGURE 6.1: RISK VERSUS REWARD OF INVESTMENTS

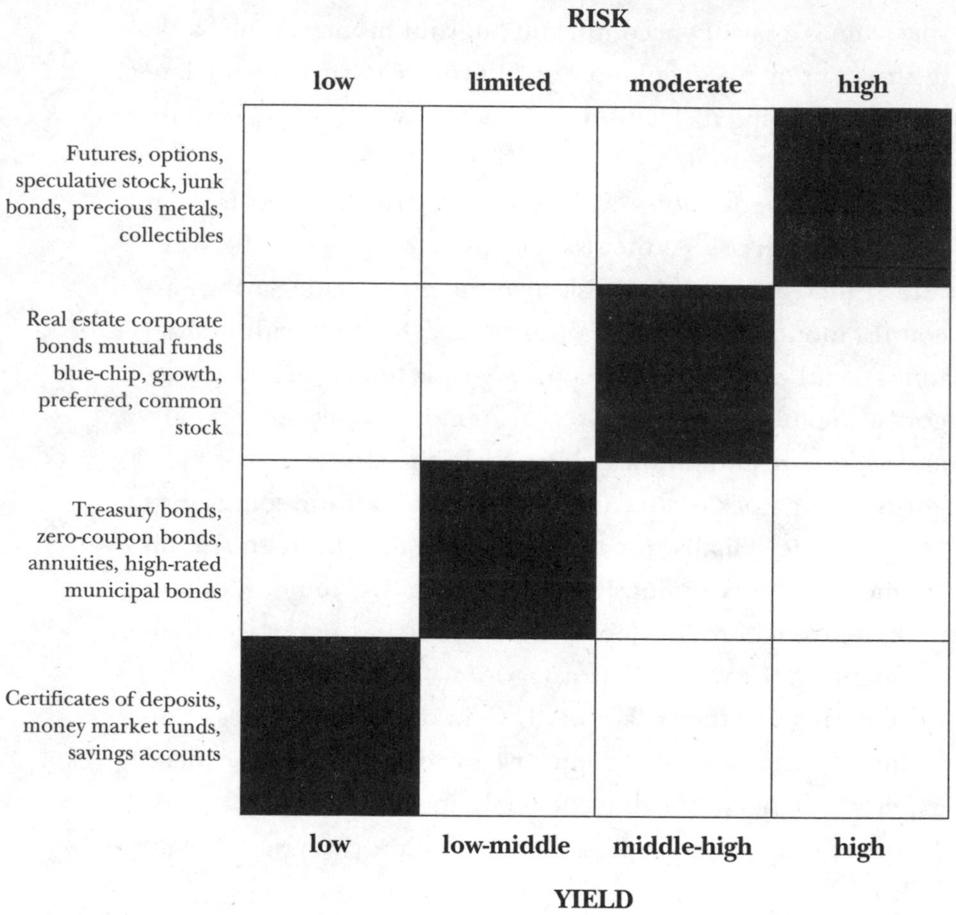

RISK

	low	limited	moderate	high
Futures, options, speculative stock, junk bonds, precious metals, collectibles				■
Real estate corporate bonds mutual funds blue-chip, growth, preferred, common stock			■	
Treasury bonds, zero-coupon bonds, annuities, high-rated municipal bonds		■		
Certificates of deposits, money market funds, savings accounts	■			
	low	low-middle	middle-high	high

YIELD

nesses develop, almost all their money goes into that development. We continued to believe that if our resources, including sweat equity, went into our farm business, it would provide for us when we could no longer be productive.

"Of course, even in our salad days, we did buy insurance and tried to maintain some cash reserves. There is a big difference between gambling and taking calculated risks. Risk-taking can be a wise part of investing when knowledge and experience are used to help you manage through uncertainty."

It's All About Balance

Investments can vary in many other ways, too. Each variation offers a chance to diversify. Remember, the more you diversify, the less risk you take for the greatest return over the long term. For example, geographic locations of investments could differ. You could invest in a mutual fund made up of foreign stocks. Or you could invest in a single corporation that does all its business in the United States. A wise investor probably would invest all over to avoid being at the mercy of any localized financial crisis.

The segment of business or society you invest in is another choice. You can pick stocks in technology companies, or you can buy entertainment industry shares. Even mutual funds can diversify in this way. Families of funds sometimes have individual funds in only one segment. (We'll describe mutual funds in the next chapter.)

The time frame of investments can vary, too. Buying a 30-year government bond is very different from buying a six-month Treasury bill.

EITHER A LENDER OR AN OWNER BE

Besides risk, there is another way of comparing ways to invest money. It boils down to one of two choices.

1. You lend your money and are paid back with interest for letting the borrower use it. The borrower may be a bank, a company, or the government. You lend your money when you deposit it in a savings account or buy a bond in a corporation or the government. Because the amount you are paid back stays the same, these are called **fixed-income assets.**

2. You buy something— stock in a company, a mobile home, a gold coin, or shares in a mutual fund— and eventually sell it at a profit. These are called **growth** *assets because they have the potential to make your investment grow.*

The point is that there are many spokes in the great wheel of diversity. To obtain a smooth financial ride, you need to pay attention to each spoke.

Diversifying, along with considering risk-reward ratios, involves having some fixed-income investments and some growth investments, some foreign and some domestic stock, some long-term and some short-term bonds. The way you divide up your money among these different *types* of assets is called *asset allocation*. It's like your financial recipe for success: You take a half cup of cash, add a pinch of speculation, three cups of growth assets like stock mutual funds, and then bind it all together with a cup of fixed-income assets. If you follow the recipe, you wind up with foolproof results every time, no matter what kind of ingredients you buy. It's the recipe—the proportions—that are the key, not so much the brand of the flour or butter or vanilla.

One other kind of asset is called a **cash equivalent.** *These investments fall into the lending category, but they are short-term loans to very solid borrowers. Examples are certificates of deposits (CDs) and Treasury bills (T-bills).*

Once you know that, you can relax about how to invest. You really don't have to spend time becoming an expert in picking out the absolutely top-performing mutual fund or trying to second-guess the stock market. You just have to keep an eye on your overall mix of assets, making sure that for each stage of life, your allocation proportions are best for you.

Ann Corley explains that her husband had some stock in the bank where he was a board member. But he also believed in diversification, Ann says, so they had money in other stocks, mutual funds, government bonds, and their home.

Since her husband's death, Ann has not altered the way the portfolio is distributed among the different investments, but she does "watch the stocks carefully and make changes when I think they are appropriate. When one of my stocks, Merck, fell 10 points, I bought another 50 shares. This is called 'down averaging.' When the stock regained its 10 points, I not only made my money back, I made extra."

What Ann Corley describes doing with her Merck stock is also known as *rebalancing* her portfolio. To use another example, say you're a 37-year-old married man, with two young children. You decide your optimum asset allocation for the next few years is 85 percent in stocks, 10 percent in bonds, and 5 percent in cash. Then suddenly there is a minicrash in the stock market. Almost everyone you know is selling all their stocks and trying to buy up bonds. If you are following our advice, you resist selling your stock. Instead, you just keep making sure your overall percentages stay the same by *rebalancing*. Sometimes that may be easier said than done.

Rebalancing in this case means you'd look at your investments and see that, because of the stock market dip, the value of your stock now accounts for 50 percent of your investments, while your bonds are doing so well they are worth 45 percent of your total investments. What you would need to do next might seem to go against human nature: You'd sell bonds and buy stock until you were back to your original 85–10 percent ratio. This is nothing more than another old-fashioned, tried-and-true technique for investing wisely: *Buy low, sell high.*

A similar important concept is *dollar cost averaging*. It means that for the periodic investment you make—say, monthly—you decide on your allocation and remain faithful to it no matter what the stock or bond markets are doing. If stock prices go down, then the same amount of money will buy more shares on the cheap. If stocks go up, then the value of your holdings goes up. You can do this with monthly investments in stocks, mutual funds, annuities, and the like. Figure 6.2 depicts dollar cost averaging.

FIGURE 6.2: DOLLAR COST AVERAGING

Price

Investment Purchases

Your regular investment would purchase the following shares:

Investment Purchase	Amount Invested	Price	Shares
1	$500	10	50
2	500	8	62
3	500	6	83
4	500	5	100
5	500	8	62
Totals	**$2,500**		**357**

In this example, the average price per share is $7.40, yet your average cost was only $7 per share. This is because when the price was high, you bought fewer shares, and when it was low, you bought more shares. Like any investment strategy, dollar cost averaging doesn't guarantee a profit or protect against loss in a declining market. Because dollar cost averaging requires continuous investment regardless of fluctuating prices, you should consider your financial and emotional ability to continue the program through both rising and declining markets.

Source: A.G. Edwards

One financial planner puts it this way, "Time, not timing, is the key. Decide what asset allocation makes sense for you and stick with it. Trying to time the market and moving into or out of certain assets based on short-term conditions is a sure-fire way to consistently underachieve."

If you follow this principle, you will keep earning money on your investment. If you follow your human nature, you naturally will want to get rid of investments that are doing poorly and hang on to those that are making money like mad. But in the long run, you will lose your money when you buy high and sell low. And planning for a comfortable financial future means planning for the long haul.

When to Rebalance Versus When to Recalculate

Rebalancing is different from recalculating your asset allocation. You probably need to rebalance about once a year or even more often, but you should think about your asset allocation whenever your financial situation changes very much. For example, the following circumstances usually affect a family's finances dramatically and call for an asset allocation review:

- Marriage
- Birth of a child
- Buying a house
- Children starting college
- Divorce or death in the family
- Changing jobs or starting a business

In Carnell's case, the circumstances that changed her and her husband's asset allocation was realizing that as their children developed their own careers, none of them was going to take over the family farm business. "This meant we needed to turn our farm investment into nonfarm assets as part of our retirement plan," Carnell says. "We have a '10-Year Lease—Option to Buy' plan for the pork production facilities. During this period, the person leasing the farm operates the farm business, and we receive a percentage of the market value of the hogs.

"We've worked with consultants and a professional financial planner to initiate this plan. We visualize a pyramid-shaped diagram, with the highest-risk investments at the top and the low-risk investments at the bottom. For retirement, we hope to create a nice broad, secure base for that pyramid with less emphasis on the top. Right now, more than a third of our holdings are in the top tier.

"Our goal is to take the greater portion of the money we receive from the lease payments and invest it so that in 2001, when the lease payments end, we will have enough in investments to live off the interest. Because safety is a primary goal, we're spreading the investments over mutual funds, bonds, carefully selected stocks, CDs, annuities, and local money markets. As we save, we are committed to not touching the principal."

Your Best Pie

How do you figure out your own best asset allocation? It's clear that the more extreme strategies don't offer the best return on your investment. For example, Buffy realizes she needs to change the mix of her asset allocation. Too much of her net worth is in cash right now, for some very practical reasons. She says, "My biggest problem is having to carry a large cash balance in my checking accounts. I pay pretty stiff taxes, and I need that liquidity to write quarterly checks. I also build modular homes for my customers, and when I sell one I need to pay the manufacturer upon delivery. I know I should whittle down the amount of cash I have because it's not making enough return for me. But I feel some security in keeping it. Twenty-two percent of my net worth is in cash.

"Nine percent is in personal assets that I own outright, and 59 percent is in real estate holdings. It's only recently that I have felt comfortable enough to buy stocks. About 5 percent of my portfolio is in the stock market; another 5 percent is in IRAs and life insurance."

Take a look at Figure 6.3.

You can see at a glance that if you invested 75 percent in stocks and 25 percent in bonds, your return rate would be about double the rate if you limited your asset allocation to 100 per-

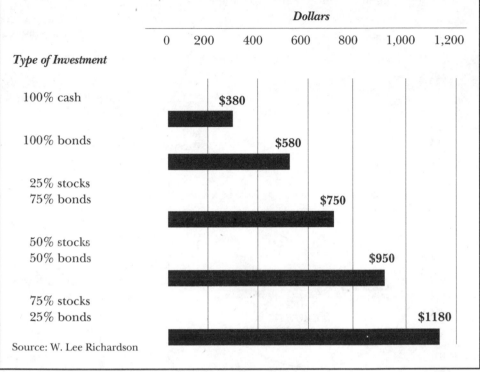

FIGURE 6.3: EFFECT OF ASSET ALLOCATION ON INVESTMENT RETURN

If you had invested $100 in 1974, this is how much it would have grown by 1994:

Dollars

| | 0 | 200 | 400 | 600 | 800 | 1,000 | 1,200 |

Type of Investment

100% cash — $380

100% bonds — $580

25% stocks
75% bonds — $750

50% stocks
50% bonds — $950

75% stocks
25% bonds — $1180

Source: W. Lee Richardson

cent cash. And although your risk rates also differ quite a bit, the actual risk is greatly reduced in an investment spread over twenty years.

Figures 6.4, 6.5, and 6.6 present three "pie charts" using a variety of "ingredients."

Once you understand your own taste in pie, you're ready to delve into one and start eating. The next chapter will describe each ingredient—or investment option—so you can bake the best pie for yourself.

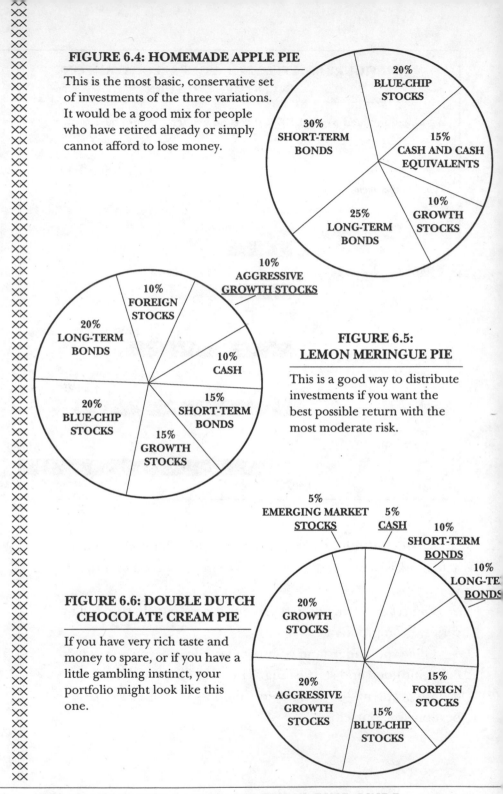

FIGURE 6.4: HOMEMADE APPLE PIE

This is the most basic, conservative set of investments of the three variations. It would be a good mix for people who have retired already or simply cannot afford to lose money.

20%
BLUE-CHIP
STOCKS

30%
SHORT-TERM
BONDS

15%
CASH AND CASH
EQUIVALENTS

25%
LONG-TERM
BONDS

10%
GROWTH
STOCKS

10%
AGGRESSIVE
GROWTH STOCKS

10%
FOREIGN
STOCKS

20%
LONG-TERM
BONDS

10%
CASH

FIGURE 6.5: LEMON MERINGUE PIE

This is a good way to distribute investments if you want the best possible return with the most moderate risk.

20%
BLUE-CHIP
STOCKS

15%
SHORT-TERM
BONDS

15%
GROWTH
STOCKS

5%
EMERGING MARKET
STOCKS

5%
CASH

10%
SHORT-TERM
BONDS

10%
LONG-TE
BONDS

FIGURE 6.6: DOUBLE DUTCH CHOCOLATE CREAM PIE

If you have very rich taste and money to spare, or if you have a little gambling instinct, your portfolio might look like this one.

20%
GROWTH
STOCKS

20%
AGGRESSIVE
GROWTH
STOCKS

15%
FOREIGN
STOCKS

15%
BLUE-CHIP
STOCKS

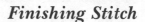

Finishing Stitch

1. DIVERSIFICATION GENER-
   ATES BETTER RETURN FOR
   LESS RISK THAN MOST
   OTHER STRATEGIES.

2. UNDERSTAND THE RELA-
   TIONSHIP BETWEEN RISK
   AND REWARD.

3. THINK IN TERMS OF ASSET
   ALLOCATION INSTEAD OF
   FOLLOWING OR TRYING TO
   SECOND-GUESS THE DAY-TO-
   DAY MARKET.

4. KEEP A WATCH ON YOUR
   PORTFOLIO PIE. BUY LOW,
   SELL HIGH.

CHAPTER SEVEN

The Long and the Short of It

RUNNING STITCH:

There's Somewhere for Everyone to Invest

"It's not how much money you make," Ann Corley's husband used to say, "it's what you do with it." Now that we have a good idea of how to think about investing, risk reward, and asset allocation, let's look at where to invest in more detail. There are three major investment areas: stocks, bonds, and mutual funds. Additional places to invest include CDs, real estate, gold, and collectibles.

In this chapter we'll define each type of investment and summarize its advantages and disadvantages. Naturally, since we're members of a stock investment club, we're partial to stocks. If you're especially interested in stocks, you might want to read our first book, *The Beardstown Ladies' Common-Sense Investment Guide.*

Stocks

A stock is a share in the ownership of a corporation. Stock is considered an "owning" or growth-income type of investment. You can invest in a broad range of businesses from multinational, very established, consistently profitable corporations such as General Electric and Pfizer, to small, grass-roots companies that go public such as Boston Chicken. A stock can cost $1, $100, or more, depending on its market value: how well it's doing, how well it's done, and how well it's expected to do in the future.

You make money in the stocks either by selling the stock for more than you paid for it or by receiving a portion of the company's annual profits, which are divided among stockholders as *dividends.*

In our minds, you just can't go wrong investing in stocks as part of your retirement plan. To show you what investing in the stock market can do, Shirley likes to tell how she purchased 200 shares of A.G. Edwards, the investment company that caters to private investors, in June of 1975. The stock was selling for 9 1/8 then, so her purchase cost $1,880.63. Without buying one additional share, today she owns 4,625 shares, worth more than $100,000.

"The extra shares came to me through stock splits and dividends," explains Shirley. "Sometimes when a company pays a dividend, it pays in the form of shares rather than cash. A.G. Edwards often pays both ways. For instance, in 1994 I received 925 shares as part of my dividend, plus dividend income of

$2,590. That cash dividend alone is worth more than my original investment."

Margaret has become such a convert, she prefers stocks to bonds now. "Before I came into the club in 1991," she says, "I bought a few bonds. At the time, I thought it was the thing to do. Now we save through stocks and mutual funds. Using the National Association of Investors Corporation low-cost investment plan, we've started our own portfolio. Each month we buy stock in McDonald's and Atmos Energy. When my bonds mature we'll take that money and invest in stocks, too."

The reason for stocks being so popular boils down to this: For long-term returns, you can't beat the risk-reward ratio of the stock market. As long as you diversify and don't buy only one company's stock, you'll come out ahead. Stock prices will go up and down, you can count on that. According to the *Wall Street Journal,* since 1926 your chances of losing money in the stock market within one year is 30 percent. But—and this is a big but—your chances of losing anything over a period of 10 years is only 4 percent.

As we wrote in our first book:

The market's history of outstanding growth is undeniable when you look at its record since the beginning of the century. Standard & Poor's 500, an index of 500 major stocks listed on the New York Stock Exchange, has plotted an overall upward trend, averaging an annual 9 percent return rate and outperforming most other investments . . . Its record is twice as good as that of corporate bonds (4.4%), Treasury bills (3.3%), and inflation (3.3%). In fact, after inflation, Treasury bills provide a zero return, in contrast to stocks which have a return of over 6 percent. The lesson of history is clear: the stock market consistently provides investors with opportunities that are difficult to match elsewhere.

We're not saying that investing in stock is a "get-rich-quick" or foolproof scheme. Nothing could be further from the truth, Carol says. "The first year I was in the club my investment actually decreased in value. When a new member joins there are startup costs that have to be figured in, plus the stocks were just not appreciating that rapidly at that time. Just as with your retirement funds, you have to be patient and let it grow."

The Balance Sheet

On the plus side:

- Stocks offer a high possible return.
- They are good for any size investment.
- Stocks are fun to pick.
- Low-fee or no-fee ways to purchase shares are available.

On the minus side:

- Stocks are too risky for short-term investment.

Bonds

Although there are several kinds, all bonds are "lending" investments: loans the investor makes to governments or corporations. Bonds fall into the fixed-income category of assets because they pay the lender a set amount of interest at set intervals of time. Buying U.S. government bonds is considered about the most solid, safest investment in the world. The downside is that bonds don't offer the rate of return of many other investments. In fact, inflation could easily turn bonds into a money-eater. If you need your money to grow, you wouldn't want to invest it all in bonds. On the other hand, to ensure you always have money, you'd probably want a portion of your assets invested in bonds, especially for something that you will need to purchase in the near future and for emergencies. And, of course, during periods where the inflation rate is zero or below—such as during severe recessions—it makes sense to buy bonds.

Here are the five main types of bonds. If after reading about them you are seriously interested in the bond market, we suggest that you get an expert's advice before making a final decision.

GOVERNMENT BONDS

Government bonds include U.S. Treasury bonds, U.S. Treasury bills and notes, and U.S. savings bonds: the kind you most likely think of when you think of bonds. Maturities can range from several months to 30 years, with longer maturities paying higher rates of interest. The catch is that if you want to sell before maturity, you might get less than the value of the bond; and the longer the maturity, the more you are subject to market risk—receiving more or less.

The Balance Sheet

On the plus side:

- You can buy government bonds directly from the Federal Reserve Bank, avoiding brokers.
- Bonds offer a high quality of credit.
- Bonds are very liquid, easy to sell.
- A wide range of prices are available, from $25 savings bonds to $100,000 Treasury bonds.
- Government bonds offer a fixed rate of interest.

On the minus side:

- They have a low rate of return.
- For those in top income tax bracket, government bonds provide a lower net income than do tax-exempt bonds.

MUNICIPAL BONDS

State and local (municipal) governments issue municipal bonds, which you buy through brokers. You don't pay federal tax on any municipal bonds and if you're a resident of the state issuing the bond, you may not have to pay state tax on it. This can make municipal bonds attractive investments for wealthier people. Like other bonds, they come in varying maturity terms and different amounts. Municipal bonds are issued for local public projects, such as new schools or water treatment plants. Beware, however, of municipal bonds whose interest payments will depend on the project they're financing making enough money. These are called *revenue bonds* because they're supposed to be paid out of future revenues. Unfortunately, while they often are used for worthwhile purposes such as hospitals, retirement homes, or low-income housing, they can be risky. Getting accurate information about municipal bonds can be difficult because municipalities are not subject to the same laws of financial disclosure as private corporations.

The Balance Sheet

On the plus side:

- Interest payments from municipal bonds are tax-exempt.

- They are good if you're in at least top third tax bracket.
- They have defined valued upon maturity.

On the minus side:

- They offer low interest rates.
- They are less liquid than government bonds.
- Municipalities are exempt from some financial disclosure laws.

CORPORATE BONDS

Corporate bonds are loans you make to corporations, at varying maturity rates. Usually these bonds require higher minimum investments than government bonds, and most corporate bonds are backed only by the corporation's ability to pay. Corporations are rated by Moody's and Standard & Poor's so you can check how solid an investment their bonds offer.

The Balance Sheet

On the plus side:

- Corporate bonds pay higher interest than Treasury bonds.
- Some, such as utilities, offer high and reliable interest payments.
- In certain tax brackets, you wind up with more money than with tax-exempt government bonds.

On the minus side:

- Interest is taxed by federal, state, and local governments.
- Corporate bonds are hard to sell before they mature.
- The corporation could default on its loan to you.

ZERO-COUPON BONDS

Zero-coupon bonds can be corporate, municipal, or Treasury bonds, sold at a much lower price than their face value. Instead of earning interest, you receive the full face value when the bond matures. In effect, the discount itself equals the interest.

The Balance Sheet

On the plus side:

- You can be sure you will have a specific amount of money at a specific time (for example, for college tuition, or a balloon loan payment).
- You will most likely stay even with inflation, although you won't increase the real value of your investment.
- If you have limited cash to invest, zero-coupon bonds are better than a regular savings account.

On the minus side:

- The interest that builds up each year is taxable, even if you don't receive it that year.
- Because prices are very unstable, you can lose money easily if you have to sell early.
- If interest rates rise, you could be stuck holding on to a low-paying investment.

JUNK BONDS

We include this category because it's *possible* that *someone* might want to invest in junk bonds. We wouldn't, but you might if you're a real gambler. Junk bonds are, as the term implies, bonds in companies that have very bad credit ratings. They are therefore quite risky. Why would anyone invest in junk bonds? Because for all that risk, you are promised high-yield returns. Of course, to get your money back with interest, you have to hope the company stays in business. Sometimes they do—MCI is one example of a junk bond that turned into a prized possession. Good luck!

Certificates of Deposit (CDs)

You buy a certificate of deposit from a bank to get a slightly higher interest rate than a plain passbook savings account. CD terms range from one month to five or more years. Although the interest rates move up and down depending on general conditions, once you buy a CD, its interest rate and therefore its value does not change.

The Balance Sheet

On the plus side:

- CDs are easy to buy.
- They entail no fees.
- Your principal is guaranteed.
- Your rate of return is guaranteed.

On the minus side:

- CDs are taxable.
- They have low interest rates—that is, low yield.

Mutual Funds

A mutual fund is managed by an investment company that gathers all the money of individual investors and then invests it in any of a number of places. A money market fund, therefore, is a mutual fund that invests in money market securities. A stock mutual fund invests in common stock. Each fund's portfolio might include anywhere from 50 to 500 different stocks or other investments. Usually a mutual fund company has a variety of "families" of funds, ranging from high-risk, aggressive, high-return stocks to more conservative, lower-interest, fixed-income funds. As a shareholder in a mutual fund, you spread your risk. Your investment in many stocks is managed by investment professionals employed by the mutual fund, so you don't have to pay as much attention to the day-to-day ups and downs of the marketplace. Instead, you pay professionals to keep an eye on the market.

An investment dream come true, mutual funds have gotten very popular in the last 20 years. At last count, more than 5,000 funds were available. They have had a dramatic impact on investing, according to many experts, because they enable those with relatively small amounts of money to enter the stock market with little risk and little cost. Before the advent of mutual funds, a small-time investor risked being wiped out by one bad stock. Now investing is much more dramatic and accessible to more people.

In addition, a lot of the "emotion" of investing is removed. Whereas you might find it hard to let go of a favorite stock, your professional mutual fund manager can evaluate each situation calmly and rationally, without any emotional attachment to individual companies.

You pay a management fee and possibly a commission to the mutual fund for handling your investment. In a front-end load mutual fund, you pay the commission "up front" when you buy your shares. In a back-end load mutual fund, you pay when you sell your shares. A no-load fund is one that does not charge a commission on your investments. But you will still pay the fee, which is built into the fund itself as a percentage. The prospectus should tell you what percentage you are being charged in fees.

Once you make your initial investment—sometimes as little as a few hundred dollars—you can buy more shares whenever you want. More and more funds offer additional shares for minimums as low as $50. There are mutual funds for investments in corporate bonds, U.S. Treasuries, municipal and foreign bonds, gold and precious metals. Within stock mutual funds, you can choose from aggressive, growth, growth and income, or international, as well as very specific individual stock areas such as health, utilities, energy, and finances. If you are really interested, take the time to go to the library and read about the multitude of funds available.

The Balance Sheet

On the plus side:

- Mutual funds offer built-in diversity of investment.
- They require low initial investment minimums.
- They are convenient.
- Professional managers run the funds.
- Automatic reinvestment takes advantage of compound interest.
- Systematic withdrawals are possible.
- Mutual funds are liquid investments.

On the minus side:

- There is some risk in investing.
- There are fees of some kind, even with "no-load" funds.
- It can be difficult to track costs to report profits and losses to the Internal Revenue Service.

Stock mutual funds are your best bet for long-term retirement investment. If you are quite knowledgeable and have the time to spend picking individual stocks on your own, then you might prefer sticking with that. But you'd probably want to invest in certain areas, such as real estate, gold, and collectibles, only if you have a lot of money, if you have some special knowledge or interest, or if you're a true gambler at heart—in which case, you probably wouldn't have picked up this book in the first place.

Real Estate

Investing in real estate can be very rewarding, but it also is tricky. You really have to be committed to spending time looking at properties, answering tenants' complaints and questions, taking care of maintenance, and praying that your property appreciates. Shirley, Buffy, and Ann Brewer have a special affection for real estate as an investment, although their stories couldn't be more different.

"There are two things I would have done differently in growing our nest egg," says Ann. "The first is, I wish we had invested in stocks when we were younger. The second is real estate. When my husband's mother passed away, he inherited a mobile home. The attorney told my husband to sell it. I said, let's rent it for a year and see what happens. We rented it to a nice gentleman who took care of it, and in time, we bought the lot the home is on. By keeping it instead of selling it, we have had the income for many years, plus we still own it.

"Meanwhile, about two years ago, we bought another house and we've done well renting it out, too. I wish we had ten more like it. There's a good rental market here in Beardstown."

Buffy couldn't agree more. "Most of my investments are in

real estate," she says, "because that is what I know. I bought my first home in 1972 when I was 19. I saved a $7,000 down payment by working throughout high school. That home is paid off now, and I take the money I get from renting it and put it toward more expensive properties.

"I purchase small, single-family homes and rent them out. Hopefully there is a positive cash flow. I let all the money I collect in rent go back into the homes in the form of mortgage payments, or maintenance and improvements, or in additional payments directly toward the principal. I recently began buying office buildings, which I rent to government agencies. They have such a good payment record!

"One of the things I like about real estate is that I'm always in control. I buy the house. I collect the rent. I take it to the bank. When something breaks, I call the plumber."

Shirley started buying land in the late 1950s when "it was dirt cheap." She saw that farmland was being taken out of production and says, "I felt that would make it more valuable. That trend continues today. Every time a cloverleaf is built, there goes another 40 acres. The truth about farmland is this: They aren't making any more.

"A good bit of my income today comes from renting out the land. I receive a share of the crops the farmers grow. One of the men I work with is Elsie's son. Some farmers wouldn't like dealing with a woman, but my tenants don't mind. They are perfectly happy if I want to go out and see how the corn is growing. I own the land in partnership with my brother, but guess who does the book work? So many of us in the club have farm interests and farm relations. Buffy says, 'We are all country gals.' "

The Balance Sheet

On the plus side:

- Real estate that is rented provides steady income.
- Rents usually go up faster than the owner's expenses.
- You gain tax breaks through depreciation.
- Property values usually rise at least at the same rate as inflation.

On the minus side:

- Real estate is not liquid.
- Real estate increases in value more slowly than other types of investments.
- Real estate investments can take up a lot of time and energy in maintenance and tenant relations.

Gold

The word "gold" may sound like something out of a fairy tale. But there are some advantages to investing in it. We suppose some people just like thinking that their money is in such a concrete, material form. There are several ways to invest in gold, ranging from purchasing actual gold bullion and gold coins, to buying gold mining stock and gold futures.

Investing in gold becomes even more appealing during unstable political or economic periods or during high-inflation cycles. That's because it is so easily sold anywhere in the world. On the other hand, it doesn't grow by earning interest. In fact, it can wind up costing you money to store or insure it.

The Balance Sheet

On the plus side:

- Gold is an excellent anti-inflation investment.
- It is the most liquid of all investments.
- It is the safest investment in an unstable political or economic situation.

On the minus side:

- Gold doesn't earn interest.
- It doesn't grow.
- It costs money to store or insure.

Collectibles

When inflation is high, more of us seem to turn to investing in objects that we collect; hence the term "collectible." Paintings, rare books, coins, stamps, baseball cards, comic books, Fabergé eggs, antique cars, quilts, jewelry are all collectible. But are all collectibles investments? Not always. You can't be sure that at the moment you decide to let go of your antique pie safe that's been in the family for hundreds of years, you will be able to find a buyer willing to pay a fair price. Or that your childhood baseball card collection, which the price guides say is worth $5,000, will sell to anyone after a year-long baseball strike has devastated fans. In other words, if you have a passion for collecting something, go right ahead and enjoy your collection. But don't count on it for your nest egg.

The Balance Sheet

On the plus side:

- People can enjoy collectibles as they invest.
- Collecting is a fun leisure-time activity.
- It is educational.
- It is a way to diversify.

On the minus side:

- Collectibles are hard to sell.
- They are not very liquid.
- You can't count on their value going up.

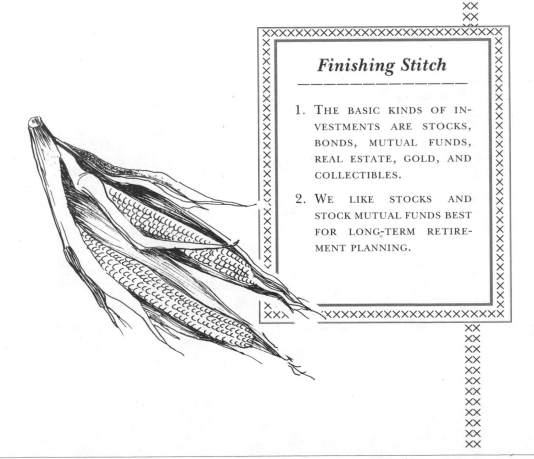

Finishing Stitch

1. THE BASIC KINDS OF IN-VESTMENTS ARE STOCKS, BONDS, MUTUAL FUNDS, REAL ESTATE, GOLD, AND COLLECTIBLES.

2. WE LIKE STOCKS AND STOCK MUTUAL FUNDS BEST FOR LONG-TERM RETIRE-MENT PLANNING.

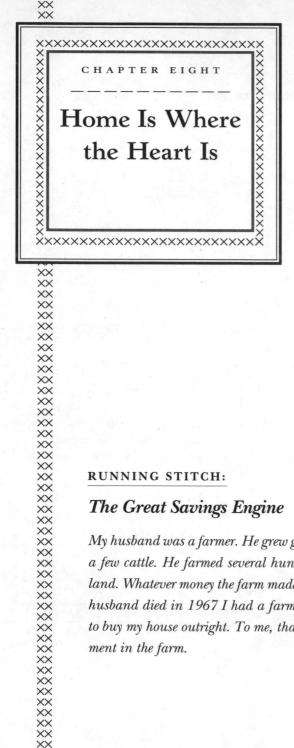

CHAPTER EIGHT

Home Is Where the Heart Is

RUNNING STITCH:

The Great Savings Engine

My husband was a farmer. He grew grain and raised purebred hogs and a few cattle. He farmed several hundred acres but we did not own the land. Whatever money the farm made went back into the farm. When my husband died in 1967 I had a farm sale, and the proceeds enabled me to buy my house outright. To me, that was a good profit from the investment in the farm.

—HELEN KRAMER

One investment that needs a chapter all to itself is owning a home. It's a completely different kind of investment from any of the others we've described. We tend to think of our house more as a place to hang our hats than a place to bank our money. When it comes to a house, we usually go with our hearts more than our minds. We fall in love with a certain look, a rosebush, a view, a neighborhood. And then we're willing to pay a lot for the security and privilege of owning that rosebush or that view, or living in that neighborhood. How else would we convince ourselves to write such hefty mortgage checks each month?

As luck would have it, buying a house may be based on emotion, but it turns out to be a good way to build part of your retirement nest, too. We know that's not the main reason Americans dream of becoming homeowners. But it's one of the biggest purchases you'll ever make, so it's nice to know that, one way or another, your house can help you financially when you retire.

First, buying a house forces you to invest a percentage of your income. No matter how strapped most people get, they manage to pay their mortgage rather than face foreclosure. Meanwhile, like the stock market, real estate generally appreciates in value over the long haul. So it's a safe bet that the house you buy today will be worth more in 30 years. At that point, you could sell it for a profit, invest the proceeds, and live on the interest. That's what Hazel did. She and her husband owned a house in Smithfield, about 30 miles north of Beardstown. When he died, she sold the house and moved to Beardstown to help take care of her mother. "The proceeds from the sale of that Smithfield house have come in handy," Hazel says. "I deposited it in a money market fund from which I have taken interest when necessary. I can even write checks on it."

If you don't sell, by the time you retire you probably will have paid off your mortgage and drastically reduced your fixed expenses by being able to live in your house rent- and mortgage-free. That's what many of the Beardstown Ladies have done.

Many of us bought our homes for a few thousand dollars. Hard to believe! Between inflation and appreciation, those houses today are worth much more. The best part, though, is that we feel so comfortable and safe in them. And, if we choose, we can afford to live in them for the rest of our lives.

Ruth and her husband, Norman, bought their house in 1946, the year after Norman was discharged from the army. It was heated by coal because gas lines had not yet been extended to that section of Beardstown. When Norman died in 1972, Ruth used one of his life insurance policies to convert the house from coal to gas. She says, "I knew neither I nor our son, Dale, who was 12 at the time, would be able to shovel all that coal. It was a major project, but I loved our home and didn't want to leave. I live in it to this day."

Sylvia and her husband bought a house in Beardstown even earlier, in 1941. "According to the bank papers," Sylvia says, "the house was built in 1895." Sylvia still lives happily in her 100-year-old home, which goes to show age isn't everything. What *should* you consider when shopping for a house?

How to Buy a House

We happen to have a professional real estate agent among our members. This is what Buffy Tillitt-Pratt tells her clients when they're thinking about buying a house:

You have probably heard this before, but it bears repeating over and over: The three most important things to consider when buying real estate are location, location, and location. No matter how neat and tidy your home is, or how nicely you can fix it up, you can't force your neighbors to be as considerate as you are about wanting a nice home and an attractive yard . . . so don't ever get into that situation where you find that perfect house located in a neighborhood of not-so-perfect homes with poorly kept lawns and shoddy exteriors. Even homes that are substantially higher in value than those surrounding them, such as the colonial two-story located on a street of 1,000-square-foot ranch homes, signifies buying a home in the wrong location. It will probably be a great bargain but as much of a bargain as it seems now, it will be equally as hard to unload on someone else—unless you sell at a bargain rate, also.

Houses in inappropriate locations appreciate more slowly, too. If you want to save money, buy a house that is the lowest-quality home in the neighborhood and fix it up while you are living there to equal the neighbors' homes. Slowly but surely, you will be increasing its value.

Another important consideration when buying a house is the structure itself. A good foundation is a must, preferably brick or concrete block. Soft brick or stone foundations mean

an older home, which may have settling and uneven floors. Solid walls and roof are also important. You want to make sure that there is no rotted or deteriorated wood from years of leaking roofs or windows. Look for water damage such as stains, peeling, cracks, and holes. Check gutters for signs of rotting. Look at the roof to see if there are any worn out shingles or bare spots. If so, you'll probably need a new roof soon.

Some people like to check rafters and walls for fire damage. This is usually not necessary. If there was a fire, the burned wood is replaced or a new board is nailed next to the burned board, which maintains the structural integrity of the home.

Mechanical equipment, which includes the furnace, air conditioning, water heater, and wiring, is very important. These items normally wear out or need updating eventually. Modern furnaces are much more efficient than older ones, and they can save dollars in fuel cost well worth the installation price. The same goes for efficient water heaters, which are relatively inexpensive compared to an old, inefficient water heater with mineral deposits on its interior walls. If you upgrade these two items, you will probably yield a good return in lower utility bills.

The wiring in a house is probably one expensive improvement that doesn't yield returns in lower utility bills—but if wiring is inadequate, you risk a major fire. Therefore, I place good wiring high on the list of improvements to look for in buying a home. If the furnace and water heater are older, you can replace them yourself and benefit in future lower utility bills. But try to find a house that already has adequate wiring.

The way to get an in-depth evaluation of the electrical, plumbing, and heating systems in a house is to hire a professional engineer or house inspector. There are a few red flags you can spot yourself:

- Does the house have enough outlets?
- Is there 220-volt wiring?
- Is the thermostat fairly new? Is it automatic?
- Is the water heater older than 12 years? Is it freestanding or a circulating system attached to a furnace?
- Is the plumbing piping made of brass, copper, galvanized iron, or PVC plastic? Are there any signs of leakage? Is the water pressure adequate?

Floor plan, size of the home, and the number of rooms are, of course, important to you. Some people say, "We can always build on." But building on rarely yields an increased sales price equal to what the addition cost. If the house you like isn't big enough or only has two bedrooms, and you need three, don't plan to add more square footage later. It will cost you more than you will gain when it comes time to sell. This advice does not pertain to finishing unused basement space if you have a dry basement. A good basement is an asset for storage now and represents cheap expansion room in the future.

One reason why people move more often rather than building on is that it is more economical to buy a new house—unless you make it a yearly habit! Even though Sylvia and Ruth have lived in their homes over 50 years, the average length of time people spend in one home is just seven years. It usually becomes too large or too small for them after that time, or they get a better job and move up or move away.

Should you buy the house you like if you think you just need to add an extra bath or redo a kitchen? If a house isn't your perfect home, you may still want to buy it and then change it somewhat to fit your need. Figure 8.1 shows approximate values that many common house improvements will yield when you get ready to sell, according to the National Association of Realtors. The key here is that too much "change" will cost more than spare change and will not return your investment when it is time to sell.

The least important consideration in buying a home is the decor. You can always add new carpet, wallpaper, and paint ... don't worry if the former owners have bad taste. If their house seems ugly on the surface, it may mean a lower sales price for you. You can feather your nest as you live in the house. Then your sweet cozy nest will provide a comfortable cushion of home equity through the combination of decreasing the amount you owe the bank while increasing its market value.

Recapping what Buffy feels is most important when buying a house:

1. Location
2. A good foundation, structure, and wiring
3. The correct size to fit your needs and lifestyle

Mortgages

Once you've found the house you think is right for you, you need to find the money to buy it. These days that almost always means borrowing most of it in the form of a mortgage. A mortgage is a loan that you repay a little at a time over 15 or 30 years. You can get a mortgage from a bank, credit union, mortgage company, mortgage broker, developer, or even the person selling the house.

Naturally, you don't get to borrow this money for free. You pay fees. You pay points. You pay closing costs. And then you pay interest on the borrowed amount—a lot of interest. But if you

FIGURE 8.1: HOW MUCH YOU GET BACK ON REMODELING

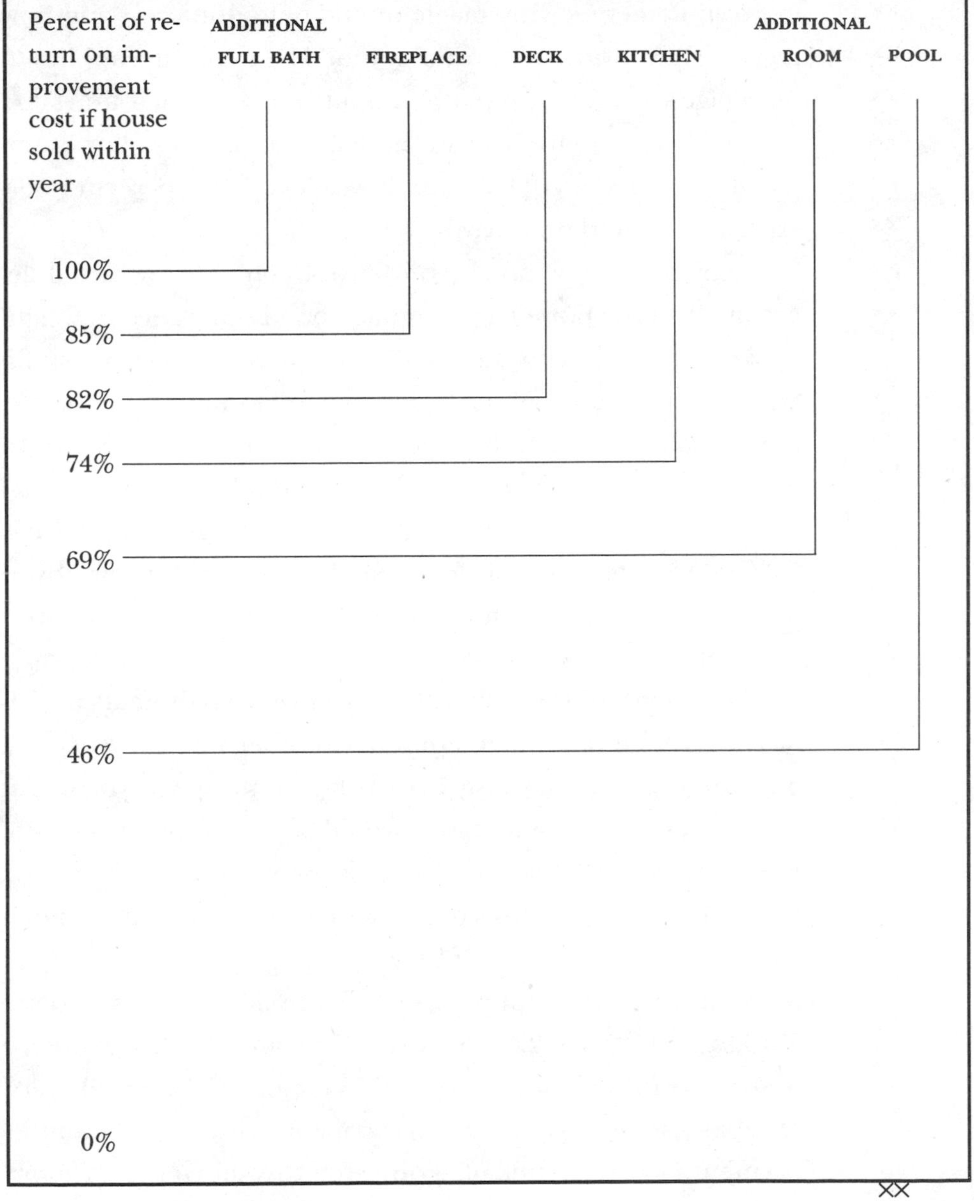

Percent of re-
turn on im-
provement
cost if house
sold within
year

	ADDITIONAL				ADDITIONAL	
	FULL BATH	FIREPLACE	DECK	KITCHEN	ROOM	POOL

100% ————

85% ————

82% ————

74% ————

69% ————

46% ————

0%

pay rent your entire life, you are effectively paying 100 percent interest. Remember the magic of compound interest and how it can help your money grow for you? The same rule applies to mortgages: You end up paying about two and a half times the original loan amount back to the lender in interest. For example, if you borrow $100,000 for 30 years at an 8.5 percent interest rate, you wind up repaying $276,808.

Remember how much your investment return varied according to a fraction of a percentage point difference in the interest it earned? With mortgages the difference between 8.25 and 8.75 percent—as many harried first-time home buyers know—can be thousands of dollars over 15 or 30 years, not to mention substantially lower or higher monthly payments. The difference between 8.5 and 10 percent interest on a 30-year $100,000 mortgage, for instance, is $109 a month. Now, if you invested that $109 in a mutual fund at 8 percent . . . well, you get the idea.

The length of the loan, called the *term,* also dramatically affects your total repayment amount. In other words, if you take out a 30-year mortgage instead of a 15-year mortgage, you might guess that your repayment total would be exactly twice as much. But, because of the nature of interest, the 15-year mortgage actually would cut your costs by more than 39 percent. How much money is that? Taking our $100,000 mortgage at 10 percent interest, in 15 years you'll pay $193,430. In 30 years you'll spend $315,925. (That's $122,495 more.) Yet your monthly payments over those 15 years would be $1,075 versus $878 over 30 years. Obviously, if there's any way you can manage the higher monthly payment, you're better off going for the shorter-term mortgage—unless, of course, you have the self-discipline to invest the $197 difference each and every month.

A whole menu of mortgages is available, including fixed rate, adjustable, graduated payment, growing equity, seven-year adjustable, balloon, and reverse mortgage. But most are variations of the two main types: fixed rate or adjustable rate.

A *fixed-rate mortgage* sometimes is called a conventional mortgage. The interest rate, amount of monthly payments, and pretty much everything else is set, or *fixed,* at the time you buy your home. You pay the exact same amount every month for the 15-, 20-, or 30-year term of the mortgage. You know from the beginning what you'll pay, how much it will cost you in interest, and how long your payments will last.

An *adjustable-rate mortgage* is often referred to as an ARM. A relatively recent innovation, an ARM is a mortgage with an interest rate that changes. It can go up or down, depending on overall variations in the economy. At regular intervals—once every year or so—the lender can *adjust* the interest rate according to a specific set of measures. Often the measure, called the index, is tied to the cost of other investments, such as the rate for U.S. Treasury bills. The adjustment can't be more than a certain limit, or *cap,* for the life of the mortgage.

There are distinct advantages and disadvantages of fixed-rate and adjustable-rate mortgages. The type you choose will depend on how much cash you have available for a down payment; what the interest rates are at the time you buy; your qualifying income; and how much you can afford in monthly payments now versus how much you think you'll be able to afford in the future.

Buffy especially encourages her clients to seek out a biweekly mortgage. Instead of paying once a month, you pay half your monthly mortgage every other week. This turns out to be 26 payments a year, or 13 "monthly" payments. The advantage of paying that one extra month's worth of mortgage can be dramatic:

	Fortunately	**Unfortunately**
Fixed-rate mortgage	You know your payment amount.	Your monthly payment may be large.
	Your monthly payment won't go up.	Closing costs may be higher.
		If interest rates go down, you'll be stuck with high payments.
Adjustable-rate	Your initial monthly payments may be low.	You can't count on what you'll be paying.
	If interest rates go down, they'll get even lower.	If interest rates go up, your monthly payments will go up, too.
	Closing costs may be lower.	The rate may become greater than the fixed rate.

On a 30-year mortgage, paying biweekly saves around seven years of payments! On a $100,000 mortgage at 8 percent interest, this would equal savings of $46,228.

Remember we said owning your home could benefit your retirement? Reverse mortgages may be a good bet if you own your home outright already and are over age 65. A reverse mortgage is really more of a home equity loan than a mortgage. You borrow a certain amount from a lending institution at a certain interest rate. Then, similar to an annuity, you receive a payment every month from a lender who adds interest to the reverse mortgage balance. Because this money is in the form of a loan, as opposed to income, it is not taxed as income and you won't become any less eligible for government benefits.

The loan is repaid in the end by selling your house, but usually not until you've moved or died. For example, if you are 66 and your house today is assessed at $100,000, you could get about $600 a month if you take out a reverse mortgage. The lender gets the money back when a prearranged time is up, when you die, or when the house is sold.

A House Is More Than a Home

When you buy a house, you have made a big investment. Even if you think you want to live there forever, it's a wise idea to look at your home from a financial point of view. There are two measures of your house as an investment: the *equity* you have in it and the different kinds of *value* of your home. Initially, equity is simply the amount of your ownership, usually the amount of your down payment: the value of the house minus the amount of mortgage. For example, if you buy a house for $100,000 and pay $50,000 in cash, borrowing the rest from a mortgage company, the equity you have in your house is $50,000, or 50 percent. Your equity will increase slowly as you pay down the mortgage. If you stay in the house until you've paid back the whole mortgage, your equity will then be $100,000, or 100 percent.

This example assumes that the value of your house does not go up or down. In real life, real estate values do vary quite a bit. Equity changes in relation to that value and whether you're talking about book or appraised value. The price you actually pay for your house is its *book value,* or its cost. It can be appraised at any time during your home ownership by a real estate agent or other professional to determine its market value. This figure can go up or down, depending on what happens to the neighborhood, the kinds of improvements you've made, and prices of other nearby homes.

For example, we know a young couple in California who bought their first home a few years ago for $100,000 with $10,000 down. Their equity was $10,000, or 10 percent. Within the next two years, they cleared out a jungle of a backyard, landscaped, painted, built a gate—and got very lucky because the whole neighborhood started improving. A nice clothing store replaced a couple of liquor stores around the corner. More families moved in to replace less stable residents. When this young couple decided to move for the sake of their careers, their house was appraised at $210,000! Their equity was now $120,000, or 57 percent.

What if they hadn't put all that "sweat equity" into their house and instead had let it deteriorate? What if the liquor stores went out of business and "for sale" signs were all that was left? No doubt the appraised value of their house would have gone down. If it dropped to $95,000, their equity would then be $5,000, or 5 percent—less than they had when they first bought the house. Likely they would have wanted to wait before trying to sell it.

Selling a House

There may come a time when you do want to consider selling your home. There are as many reasons for selling a house as for buying one. Some of them are emotional and intangible; some are more practical. Maybe your family has outgrown the size of your current house, or your children have grown and there's no reason to keep a large house. Maybe you've gotten divorced or you're moving for a new job. Perhaps when you were first married you loved Dutch Colonial, and now you want a more modern style. Could be you need to move for health reasons or a more congenial climate.

But whatever the reason, before you sign up with a real estate agent, you should realize that selling your house is more than a simple real estate transaction. It's really a financial planning decision. You need to decide whether it makes sense financially as well as for other reasons. Is it a slow market for houses? Would you get the price you want to make the hassle worthwhile? Would you have to do major improvements in order to sell it? Are you under much pressure to sell, or can you afford to wait or to take a lower price?

This is where knowing how much equity you have in your house comes in handy. Perhaps you'll decide that instead of selling, it would make more sense to remodel, rent out rooms, put in an air conditioner, or wait. If you opt to make improvements, be sure you understand which ones will increase the value of a house and which ones will just increase your comfort or pleasure. (See Figure 8.1 on p. 127.) In general, swimming pools and hot tubs don't make back their cost, whereas new kitchens, extra bathrooms, and fireplaces usually do pay for themselves in increased selling price.

Tax

Another part of financial planning in selling a home is figuring out your tax liability. Whenever you sell a house, no matter if you make or lose money on the deal, you have to declare the sale on your income tax return for that year. The Internal Revenue Service has a special form called "Sale of Your Home," it's number 2119.

Most often you will be reporting a profit, but you can't always tell at first glance. That's because your profit or loss is not based simply on the difference between how much you paid for the house and how much you are able to sell it for. It's the *adjusted basis* that concerns the Internal Revenue Service. The adjusted basis is how much you paid for the house plus how much you paid for any improvements *minus* any amount you lost while you lived there due to natural disaster or other causes.

If the adjusted basis still shows you made a profit, you don't necessarily have to pay tax right away. In fact, you can avoid paying tax on selling a home indefinitely. How do you manage that? You buy a new house within two years that costs as much as or more than the house you sold and live in it as your primary residence.

In addition, there is a once-in-a-lifetime way of avoiding taxes on selling your house, even if you don't want to buy another house. Say you've gotten to the point in your life where you want to move into a condo or a nursing home or travel around the world. If you are 55 or older when you sell, you may exclude up to $125,000 in tax on the profits. This can be a real boon to your retirement because it means you can, for this one time only, keep all the profit without paying tax on most, if not all, of it.

For example, you bought your first house 40 years ago for $10,000. You've moved three times since then and now live in a house you're about to sell for $130,000. Altogether, in selling all your homes then, you've made taxable profits of $100,000. Taking the one-time exclusion now means you can keep the profit and never pay a penny of tax on it.

The 55 and over tax exclusion offer is such a good opportunity, it makes sense to be very cagey before using it. Keep in mind, too, that married couples get only one exemption. Consult a financial expert to determine how to get the very most out of using the exclusion by timing it to your best advantage. And if you use it and then decide that was a mistake, don't worry. You can change your mind—and change your tax return—for up to three years.

Finishing Stitch

1. OWNING A HOME IS ANOTHER WAY OF PAYING YOURSELF FIRST.

2. THINK OF YOUR HOUSE AS ONE OF YOUR LARGEST INVESTMENTS: CONSIDER YOUR EQUITY.

3. TAKE ADVANTAGE OF TAX-DEFERRED PROFITS IF YOU SELL.

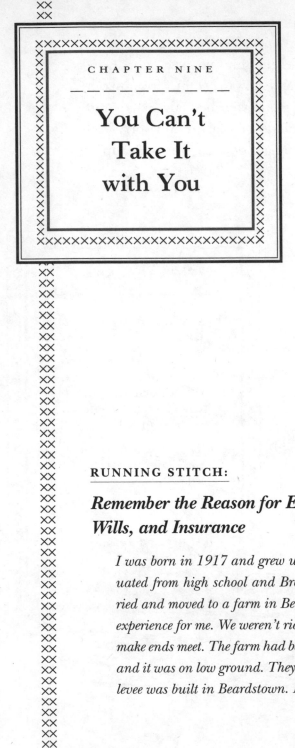

CHAPTER NINE

You Can't Take It with You

RUNNING STITCH:

Remember the Reason for Estate Planning, Wills, and Insurance

I was born in 1917 and grew up in Springfield, where I graduated from high school and Brown's Business College. I married and moved to a farm in Beardstown. Farm life was a new experience for me. We weren't rich farmers and were just able to make ends meet. The farm had belonged to my husband's father, and it was on low ground. They had lost a lot of crops before the levee was built in Beardstown. In years when the flooding was particularly bad, you could boat all the way from their house to Beardstown, a distance of two miles.

I remember one year, after the sea wall was built, there was a "dry flood." They were afraid the wall wouldn't hold the river back, and all the women and children had to leave town. But the wall did hold. You can't predict the future, so the only sensible thing to do is prepare as best you can for whatever might happen. To me, that levee represents good insurance and good planning.

—ELSIE SCHEER

There are two reasons you might not need any of the information in this chapter: if you plan to live forever or if there is no one you care about, feel responsible for, or want to help. None of us falls into the first category and very few of us fall into the second. Life insurance and estate planning aren't really about death so much as they are about those you leave behind. As long as you keep this basic idea in mind, you'll be able to make more sensible decisions about whether you even need life insurance, how much you need, what type you need, and how to pass on your assets in the most convenient, least heavily taxed way.

Financial planning for after your own death can be a very emotional subject, and it's certainly hit home for us in the past year. "We are more mindful of things now that we have lived through the death of one of our members, Lillian Ellis," Shirley states. "It is my responsibility to lead educational sessions at each meeting of the Beardstown Ladies' Investment Club. I have been stressing the importance of having an up-to-date will, for example."

Shirley describes what can happen if you don't have your business affairs in order. "My father was an attorney," she explains, "and one of his clients passed away. The nephew came in to see about his uncle's unfinished business. He had with him a key to a safe deposit box, but no one recognized it. First my father tried the Beardstown banks. Then he found a counter check in the uncle's billfold to a small bank in the county. A phone call confirmed a safe deposit box and a checking and saving account. The box had his deed to his home and farmlands, title to a truck and a car, and many more valuables. Lesson: Let someone know where your safe deposit box, key, will, checking accounts, savings accounts, and the like are held.

"Another time I was cataloging the possessions of a woman who had lived most of her life in poverty. She had passed away, and there was to be an auction. I was sorting her books. I remember picking up a copy of *Tarzan*. Money fell out. She had money in all her books. It totaled thousands of dollars.

"If you hide money, let someone that you trust know where it is. Those books could have been sold for a dollar a box!"

Estate Planning

Since many of us are widows, we have firsthand experience in the value of thinking about the future today. Ann Corley says, "As a widow, I am keenly aware of how important it is to plan carefully for the future. It's hard to think about the possibility that one partner would pass away, but if you don't prepare things can be more difficult and more costly. Often it falls on the woman because the sad truth is the men usually go first. Before my husband passed away I had never reconciled a bank statement. I had never even paid a bill. He handled all our finances. I think that was the way many women of our generation used to do.

"He knew he was dying, and we sat and talked. I think he was preparing me. It was very difficult for both of us. He had a book with all our investments in it, very well organized. Government bonds, mutual funds, all things I knew nothing about, were meticulously cataloged there. After he passed away, I would sit and study that book for hours at a time. I was learning from him even after he was gone. We both knew I would have to make the decisions someday, and now I do.

"We made sure not only our investments but possessions, such as Donald's two fishing boats, and our cars, were transferred into my name or were already in my name."

Painful as her husband's death was for Ann, the fact that her husband had thought through so many details and made sure she was well informed about their financial situation was a big help.

For many people, the word "estate" means mansions, acres of property, and millions of dollars. They assume they don't need to do any "estate" planning. But if you have *any* assets—money, stocks, real estate, life insurance, retirement benefits, or other valuables or property—you have something to leave and need to plan. The definition of estate is simply *the whole of one's possessions, especially all the property and debts left by one at death.*

The main reason for estate planning is to prevent your assets from being taxed excessively after your own death. In too many cases a family is left a substantial amount, only to discover that after the *inheritance* or state taxes, the *estate* or federal taxes, and the legal fees, there's precious little left. The more your estate is worth, of course, the more planning ahead can save your heirs money. If you have more than $600,000 in assets, it would be wise to consult a professional for estate planning strategies. That's because your estate will owe federal tax on any amount over $600,000. So it might, for instance, make more sense to give your loved ones gifts of money before you die.

This plan has two advantages. First, annual gifts up to $10,000 are not taxed. Second, you can reduce the size of your estate during your lifetime to under $600,000. The whole amount then will be free of estate tax. For example, let's say you are a 70-year-old whose assets total $700,000. You have two children. You can give them each gifts of $10,000—tax-free—every year for six years. Then when you die, they won't pay estate tax either because by then your estate will be worth less than $600,000. Isn't that a nice solution to a not very nice problem?

This is a simplified version of what for most people is a much more complicated strategy. Even if you don't think you have enough of an estate to worry about, again we suggest you get professional advice. It's surprising how quickly your assets add up. Meanwhile, filling in the Estate Planner worksheet on pp. 215–217 is a step in the right direction.

Wills

Only three out of 10 Americans have a will when they die. That means the friends and family of those other seven people have to deal with a difficult situation. If you die without a will, you die *intestate*. And if you die intestate, it means state law decides what happens to your estate and, even worse, what happens to your children if they're still minors. So if you have young children, it's especially crucial to have a will. Even if your children are grown, it's much better for you to decide before your death how you want your possessions to be distributed. Your friends or business partners or favorite charities won't see a penny of your money if you die without a will.

After Lillian Ellis's death, for example, we were especially careful to designate who should receive our share of the club portfolio in the event of our death, and we filed these designations with our bylaws.

So how do you go about preparing your will? It's *possible* to do it yourself, using computerized forms or a good book. But the least little mistake can make a will invalid. We recommend you hire an attorney to help you. It shouldn't take very long and, therefore, shouldn't cost too much. Also, since the legalities vary a lot from state to state, having an attorney who is familiar with your state's law is important.

To save time in your lawyer's office—and their time is your money—you can think about answers to the following questions before your appointment. No matter what state you live in, you need to know:

- Who will be your *beneficiaries?* Who will receive a portion of your estate?
- Who will be your *executor?* Who will make sure your estate is distributed according to the terms in your will?
- Who will be your *trustee?* Who will do the hands-on management of any money you leave?
- Who will be your children's *guardian?* Who will your children live with if they are still minors when you die?

Once you've made these key decisions, you'll be able to meet with an attorney and, in just one session, provide all the information necessary for him or her to draft your will. The cost should be between $100 and $500, depending on where you live in and how complex a will you need. A typical will for a middle-age Chicago man, married with children and with modest assets, cost $300. We reprint sections of it in Appendix B, but be warned: You can't copy it and think you've got a valid will. It would have to be notarized, witnessed, and checked by a lawyer.

As your circumstances change, you'll want to revise your will. For example, if you have more children, divorce, or remarry, or if those you've named executors, trustees, or guardians move or become ill, your will should reflect these changes. Meanwhile, be sure to let those involved know where a copy of your will is kept. It doesn't do your heirs much good to have a will if they can't find it or don't know your attorney. Your executor can keep a copy in his or her own safety deposit box. Depending on your state law, you can keep the original in your lawyer's office vault or in a safekeeping service provided by many banks.

If for any reason you do not have a will drafted by a lawyer, writing one by hand is better than no will at all. If it can be proven that you really wrote it yourself, it is legally valid. It should be witnessed by two people, neither of whom are beneficiaries. While we do recommend going to a lawyer, a *holographic* will, as handwritten wills are called, is a last resort that helps you to avoid dying intestate.

Perhaps a better way to save legal fees and lots of time is by keeping good records. This is often much easier said than done. It's amazing how much we all own when we start really thinking about our property. Remember our midwestern farmer and his wife who retired so comfortably in Chapter 1? Not surprisingly, they also are great at keeping track of their "estate," down to the details. Here is a letter they sent to each of their sons recently:

Dear Son,

We are sending you some information about our financial status and personal possessions. We probably should have done this a long time ago since you and Bill are co-executors of our estate. We don't have a whole lot, but we want you to be aware of what we do have. Please read this over and call us if you have questions about anything. Be sure and keep the fact sheet for future information. I'm sending identical information to your brother.

Lots of love to all of you,
Mom

THE FACTS*
    Finances
      IRAs—City Bank
        Dad's (larger because of Dairy Retirement)
        Mine
      Checking Accounts
        Federal Savings Bank
          1. Account number 0-10-06-143278
          2. Account number   0-10-06-154923 (Farm account)
      Savings Accounts
        City Bank
        Federal Savings
      Mutual Benefit Pension Plan
      Certificates of Deposit
        Bank of Indiana

*All names, amounts, account numbers, and details have been changed.

1. Number 0042117227 ($5,000)
2. Number 1142012868 ($2,173.68)

Johnson Dairy Stock

Johnson Dairy has been sold to Smith Dairy

250 shares @ $18/share = $4,500

Savings Bonds

State Bank

$100 bonds (1984–1992) = 103

One $1,000 bond

Safety Deposit Box

Our key is in bottom of Pie Safe, under blanket

State Bank: Has CDs, savings bonds, etc.

Pink arrowhead for Tom; white arrowhead for Bill

$5 gold piece, Dad's from his aunt and uncle upon graduation from high school, 1943. Valuable. Maybe Bill should have this, since Joel and Lynn have college bonds.

Farm

Dad thinks farm is worth $2,000–$3,000/acre. Sixty-eight acres of farmland and 12 acres of woods. Title and abstract in safety deposit box.

Crops

Ear corn stored in barn loft and outside bin. Henry Allen has been buying it and hauls it to Kentucky.

Wheat is usually harvested around July 4.

Insurance

$5,000 life insurance policy at the Dairy.

Three $1,000 policies in safety deposit box.

New Ford Tractor purchased in November 1993. Paid with cash.

Magazine Subscriptions

We take *Time* (expires Feb. 1997), *Readers Digest* (Dec. 97), *Farm Journal,* (Dec. 97) and *Country Living* (Oct. 96). *Good Housekeeping* runs out in June.

More information can be found in the small blue file cabinet in my closet.

Living Wills and Power of Attorney

These days, as medical advances postpone or confuse the end of life, it's very important to have a living will and a durable power of attorney in place. The time to think about these documents is *before* you become mentally or physically disabled. A living will tells your doctors, hospital, and family what you would like done in different medical situations. For example, some people do not want to be kept alive on a life support system after a certain point or if their mental abilities have deteriorated. This is a new, somewhat gray area in terms of the law, so such a document may not be as strong legally as a regular will. But at least your family won't have to try to guess what you would have liked at the same time they're coping with their grief.

You can get living will forms from your lawyer, many doctors' offices, and retirement and nursing homes.

Along the same lines, a durable power of attorney for health care makes a specific person responsible for decisions about your medical care if you can no longer make those decisions. Many hospitals now insist patients name someone before they can be admitted. A standard durable power of attorney gives someone the authority to act legally on behalf of a person who has become incapacitated. The power of attorney has to be created while you are still mentally alert, however. Then whoever you name can pay your bills and take care of any other necessary business for you when the time comes.

Life Insurance

When a person is left widowed or orphaned, one of the first questions everyone asks is "Did they receive any life insurance?" The second question is invariably "How much?" A lot of those who need life insurance do not have any. And those who do usually don't have nearly enough. On the other hand, there are many people who pay hefty premiums for completely unnecessary life insurance. Those insurance salesmen can be so persuasive! In the face of an aggressive or guilt-inducing sales pitch, how do you know whether you should buy insurance? You probably should say no until you've had time to assess your individual needs. You may not need much life insurance if you fall into one of the following categories:

- You are not married and have no children or others you support.
- You have grown children who can take care of themselves financially.
- You are married but do not work.
- You are a college student.
- You are married and retired, with adequate Social Security, pension, and savings to support your spouse in the event of your death.

But if:

- You are married and have young children *or*
- You are not married but you support or help support someone *or*
- Your estate is over $600,000 and there will be estate tax *or*

- You are married, have no children, but your spouse does not work *or*
- You are married, you both work, but your spouse would not be able to live in the style to which he or she has become accustomed if you were to die,

then you *do* need to carry life insurance, although how much you need to purchase will vary according to individual circumstances. Insurance is like sunscreen. Before you need it, any amount seems unnecessary. But after you need it, any amount seems like too little.

Elsie explains that her husband was a good planner. She's grateful that he always looked ahead. "He bought quite a bit of insurance even though I was against his buying so much. When he passed away in 1978, all that money we had been paying in over the years became my nest egg. I was so thankful to have it."

So how do you figure out how much you need? There are some basic rules of thumb, but even they vary all the way from five times to 11 times your annual salary. A better method is to fill out a worksheet with more specific numbers. You need to calculate the amount of money necessary to fill the gap between your income and whatever other sources of support your family may receive. We include a simple Insurance Planner form on p. 218 in Appendix A, or you can work with a good insurance planner.

After doing this calculation, chances are you will decide you need to increase your insurance coverage. Every now and then, however, the opposite may be true. When Margaret and her husband reevaluated their insurance policies, they decided they had too much monthly income going into insurance. "All we could see was hundreds and hundreds of dollars going down the drain," she says. "One of the policies we cut down on was health insurance. We felt it was inflated. We took a lesser policy with a higher deductible. Now that money is being invested in stocks. And we're praying we stay healthy."

Sadly, we can't always count on that, as Maxine knows all too well. This is her story: "For our 40th wedding anniversary, the boys wanted us to have a reception. Roy said, 'No, Mom and I are going to Europe. I don't want to shake hands with a lot of people who couldn't care less.' We had a wonderful trip, going to Austria, Switzerland, and Germany. I'm so thankful for our trip and memories. We got home in October 1980 and he died at the end of December.

"When I received Roy's life insurance check, I thought, 'My goodness, I have to invest this.' Fortunately I had been involved with the Business and Professional Women's Club for 20 years, had joined the investment club, and using this knowledge I felt I could handle it.

"That insurance money eventually wound up in mutual funds, stocks, CDs, and Treasury bills, where it grows to this day. I didn't want to put all my eggs in one basket. Once in a while, I take some of the interest and go on a trip, but I don't touch the principal."

Choosing Life Insurance

There are three basic types of life insurance: term, whole, and universal. Term life insurance is the least expensive and most straightforward option. It provides a predetermined death benefit for a set period—*term*—of your policy. After the term is up, you can renew your coverage but at a higher premium rate. Term insurance is good when you are young and your income may be a bit tight. For a reasonable amount, you can protect your family without undue strain on your budget. It's the bread and butter of life insurance.

For a higher price, you can buy whole life or straight life, also known as cash-value life insurance. These policies do double duty as both a death benefit and as an investment instrument. You pay a premium that doesn't change and is set according to your age at the time you purchase the policy. The older you are, the higher the premium rate. The other big difference between it and term insurance is that the company pools your premium payments into a savings fund and invests a portion of it. These earnings are tax-deferred. Gradually the *cash value* of your policy increases through your own contributions and the company's earnings on its investments. If you want, you can surrender the policy—before you die—and walk away with the cash it's worth (although you will pay taxes on the amount you cash in less the total premiums paid in). Or you can borrow against the value of the policy without paying taxes and without canceling your coverage. However, you will owe taxes on the amount over what you paid in. Also, because the yield—the interest rate you receive—is relatively low, you can often save more through noninsurance investment programs. Usually you don't have any say over how your insurance money is invested; however, many variable whole life policies now let you choose from among several investment options (stocks, bonds, money markets, etc.).

Universal life is a more flexible form of a cash-value life insurance policy. You can adjust the premiums as well as the amount of the death benefit during your lifetime. In other words, you can decide how much of the premium is going toward life insurance and how much is going toward accumulating cash. You even can change when you pay the premium. Of course, this flexibility may come at a price. Although you can change your premiums, the company can change your coverage. So if interest rates go down, for example, the company will likely increase your premiums if you want to maintain the amount of coverage you previously had.

A newer variation of universal life is the variable universal life policy. It's like a universal life policy, but you purchase mutual funds within the insurance contract. Also, you pay monthly premiums, so your cost is taken out on a monthly basis. That means more of your money is working in a mutual fund investment for a longer period of time than if you were paying premiums annually or semiannually.

Look at this comparison chart of life insurance policies.

How *can* you compare the overall costs of life insurance polices? It might seem like apples and oranges, but luckily you can obtain something from insurance companies called an *illustration,* which details costs and values projections using different assumptions. We suggest you use more than one life insurance salesperson to supply the information. That way you'll get a

	Premium	Cash Value	Purpose
Whole	Fixed amount	Some	Death benefit for survivors; investment, lower rate of return
Term	Cheapest at first; then increases at end of each term or annually	None	Death benefit only
Universal Life	Variable	Varies	Death benefit; investment with moderate rate of return
Variable Universal Life	Variable	Varies	Possible higher rate of return

more diverse range of choices to analyze. Keep in mind, too, that the length of time that the coverage will be needed is important in deciding which makes the most sense. The longer you will need it—say, greater than 10 or 15 years—the more attractive a cash value policy will be. Again, a good insurance planner or an accountant should be able to help design a policy that best fits your circumstances.

If you would like a detailed analysis of how policies compare, you can pay a small fee to the National Insurance Consumer Organization to evaluate whatever your agent suggests. Their address is listed in the Resources section at the end of this book.

In addition to checking out policies, you will want to look up the company's record. Again, there is a handy way to do this because insurance companies are given report cards by several independent organizations. They can receive anywhere from a *superior* to a *nonviable* rating. It's pretty obvious that there's no reason not to go for a top-rated company if you have any choice at all. Depending on the rating organization, the superior grade could look like an A+, AAA, or Aaa. Table 9.1 shows how the three main ratings companies grade insurers.

Should you want to contact the assessing organizations directly, their phone numbers are as follows: Standard & Poor's

Table 9.1: Ratings Systems for Life Insurance Companies

	S&P	A.M. BEST	MOODY'S
Superior Nearly risk-free, very solid company	AAA	A+	Aaa
Excellent Almost risk-free, almost as good as superior	AA+ AA AA–	A+ A A–	Aa1 Aa2 Aa3
Good Solid company with slight degree of risk	A+ A A–	A– B+	A1 A2 A3
Adequate Okay financially, some risk	BBB+ BBB BBB–	B B– B–	Baa1 Baa2 Baa3
Below Average Fairly weak, some speculative risk	BB+ BB BB–	C+	Ba1 Ba2 Ba3
Weak Very vulnerable and risky	B+ B B–	C C–	B1 B2 B3
Nonviable High risk of not meeting financial obligations	CCC CC, D		Caa Ca, C

212-208-1527; Moody's 212-553-0377; A.M. Best 900-555-2378 (Note: You will be charged extra for this 900 number). It's a good idea to take advantage of the knowledge backing these ratings. Why bother buying low-grade life insurance when it's easy to find out which policies are high-grade?

Finishing Stitch

1. ESTATE PLANNING IS VALUABLE FOR EVEN MODEST ASSETS.

2. IT'S IMPORTANT FOR THE SAKE OF YOUR LOVED ONES THAT YOU LEAVE A WILL.

3. BE SURE YOU REALLY NEED LIFE INSURANCE.

4. SHOP AROUND FOR THE MOST SENSIBLE LIFE INSURANCE COVERAGE FOR YOUR SITUATION.

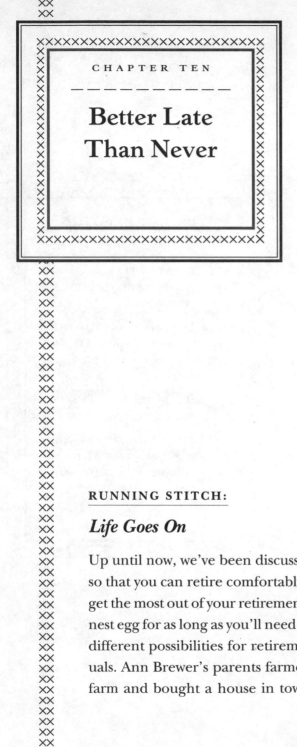

CHAPTER TEN

Better Late Than Never

RUNNING STITCH:

Life Goes On

Up until now, we've been discussing how to grow your nest egg so that you can retire comfortably. This chapter is about how to get the most out of your retirement years and how to protect your nest egg for as long as you'll need it. Of course, there are as many different possibilities for retirement living as there are individuals. Ann Brewer's parents farmed all their lives, then sold the farm and bought a house in town. Her father died shortly afterward, and her mother began drawing Social Security and worked part time in a lawyer's office. "Between those two, and the fact that she owned her home," Ann says, "she has been able to make a go of it."

In her years working at the bank, Helen Kramer counseled many people, especially women, who wanted to retire but didn't have much to retire on. "Women tend to put everyone ahead of themselves," says Helen. "It's a wonderful quality but not good for a secure retirement. They are willing to sacrifice for other things, such as their children's education, but it often leaves them alone and with little to live on. On average, women make 24 percent less than men and live seven years longer. They have to make less money go farther. Retirement can be more difficult for women than for men."

Helen herself relics on her annual pension and IRAs. "I have adequate money to live on," she says. "Depending on my expenses, I sometimes have additional money, which I can invest in my stock portfolio. I still have some CDs and cash savings that I would go to if I needed or wanted something beyond my monthly income."

Figure 10.1 presents an example of how one retired Beardstown Lady has her investments divided.

FIGURE 10.1 POST-RETIREMENT PORTFOLIO

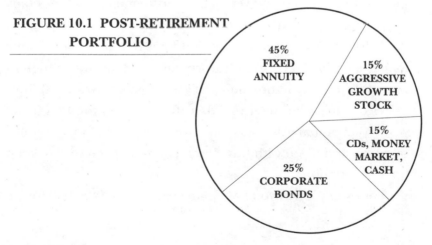

45%
FIXED
ANNUITY

15%
AGGRESSIVE
GROWTH
STOCK

15%
CDs, MONEY
MARKET,
CASH

25%
CORPORATE
BONDS

Your Investments After Retirement

Helen is smart to continue investing and to stay diversified during her retirement years. It's good to keep some money invested for growth because you never know whether inflation will rear its head and eat up your "savings." Resist the temptation, once you stop working, to put all your money into such "safe" investments that it won't last through your lifetime. And beware: Your lifetime might last longer than you think, if statistics are any gauge. Today, according to the United States Census Bureau, there are 3,638,000 Americans 85 years old and over. Thirty-five years ago only 947,000 Americans were that age. By 2025 there will be 7,038,000 Americans in the 85 and older age group. Even more dramatic, today there are 54,000 people 100 years old and over. In 30 short years, that figure will be 360,000!

But counting on living until you're a centenarian is probably unrealistic for most of us. In terms of retirement money, it's too late to start investing in some scheme that promises great wealth in, say, another 50 years. If someone comes knocking on your retirement home door trying to sell you a limited partnership in oil wells, common sense says just say no.

You need to stay focused on the solid investment practices that we've discussed and yet feel free to spend enough to enjoy your retirement. You've been saving all those years for *these years,* don't forget! You want to be able to get the most out of your longer life without constantly worrying about having enough to live on. To figure out how much of your capital you can withdraw to live on each year, refer to Table 10.1. It shows you how many years your capital will last if you have it invested at various rates of return and if you withdraw 4 percent more each year to keep up with inflation.

For example, say you have managed to save $400,000 for re-

Table 10.1: How Long Will Your Money Last?

Money invested will last for the number of years where the rate of return intersects with that percent of capital you take out annually (the figures running down the left-hand column).

		AVERAGE RATE OF RETURN						
		4%	**5%**	**6%**	**7%**	**8%**	**9%**	**10%**
Percent of	2%	50	68	151	*	*	*	*
capital you	3%	33	40	52	96	*	*	*
withdraw	4%	25	28	34	42	69	*	*
each year	5%	20	22	25	29	36	53	*
with a	6%	17	18	20	22	25	31	43
4% inflation	7%	14	15	16	18	20	23	27
rate	8%	13	13	14	15	16	18	20
	9%	11	12	12	13	14	15	17
	10%	10	10	11	12	12	13	14
	11%	9	9	10	10	11	11	12
	12%	8	9	9	9	10	10	11

tirement in a combination of investments, and the average rate of return on your investments is a conservative 7 percent. Factoring in an inflation rate, your money will last you 29 years if you withdraw 5 percent, or $20,000 a year. That, together with Social Security and other income, should be enough to let you relax however you like.

If it *doesn't* look as if your capital is going to last long enough for your expected lifetime, you'll need to make some adjustments. You could try to invest it at a higher rate of return, lower your expenses, or earn more money. (In the Resources section, we've listed several books on part-time work during retirement.)

In making these calculations, remember to think about what you always wanted out of your retirement. Refer back to Chapter 1, when you were daydreaming about this period of your life. How close to those dreams are you? Maybe looking at a sunset over the lake seemed like a good idea when you were 40, but now it sounds boring. Maybe you realize you always wanted to learn Russian, square dance, or see Kenya. What adjustments might you make to reach your retirement lifestyle?

Are You Ready?

In the year or so before your retirement date, you should ask yourself very specific questions and gather certain information. First and foremost, you need to get your financial house in order. Do this by calculating your net worth based on all your investments, the same way you figured it out in Chapter 3. Include savings accounts, money market funds, mutual funds, stocks, IRAs, pensions, real estate, life insurance, annuities, Keoghs, and CDs. Next, try to estimate your financial needs after you retire. How much income will you have to live on? What will your expenses total? As before in your life, you need to have a spending plan in place so you know what you can and cannot afford once you are living a life of relative ease.

Now you need to look at the state of your physical well-being. Start by finding out what health care costs. Think of a range of possibilities, depending on best and worst cases. Do you know what Medicare will cover? Do you have a policy that will fill any gaps? (These are called Medigap insurance policies.) How long would your money last if you need home health care or nursing home care? Do you understand Medicaid requirements?

If you are the type who needs to check as you go, here is a handy retirement readiness reminder checklist.

- ✔ Find out the exact date you are eligible to retire.
- ✔ Recheck your Social Security estimate of benefits, your current pension plan information, and any other sources of postretirement income.
- ✔ If you have a choice, decide how you want your pension plan distributed: lump sum or annuity. (See next section for more information.)
- ✔ Before you sell a house or cash in IRAs, consult an accountant to see if you can avoid a major tax bill.
- ✔ Update your will and establish an estate plan, if you haven't done so already.
- ✔ Estimate your monthly budget.
- ✔ Make adjustments in your investments to make up for any shortfall.
- ✔ If you want to work part time or freelance, start making inquiries.
- ✔ Start cleaning and sorting your belongings if you are moving.

> *When I retire, I'm certain I'll be able to pay monthly expenses from my teacher's pension and Social Security. Interest from the other investments will enable me to do additional things, such as travel. Maybe I should say, if I retire.*
>
> **—Doris Edwards**

As the date of your retirement draws closer, you will have to deal with some paperwork. Be sure to get any records, financial statements, or health benefits from your employer *before* you leave. Get a complete physical while you are still fully covered by company health insurance. Begin looking into health insurance to fill the gap between what Medicare will cover and what you might need. Reduce or cash in your life insurance coverage. It might be better to start *using* the money you used to pay in premiums or to give it directly as a gift to any remaining dependents. Alternatively, you could convert cash values into an annuity to supplement your income. The balance can be given to close relatives. Three months before your retirement date, apply for Social Security. It can take awhile for the paperwork to go through. For Medicare, apply three months before your 65th birthday.

How to Take Your Money Out

If retirement plans were a bowl of cherries, when it came time to eat them, you'd just pick them out of the bowl one by one as you got hungry. But life and pensions are not so simple. When you pass the magic age of 70 1/2, you *have* to decide how to withdraw your carefully planned retirement funds. With most plans, you *may* withdraw money without a penalty starting at age 59 1/2. These include pension plans, Keoghs, 401(k) plans, and profit-sharing plans. Usually your choice is between receiving a *lump sum* distribution or an *annuity*. When you opt for a lump sum, you'll get a chunk of money all at once, which will be taxed. If you choose an annuity, you get a portion of your payout each month for the rest of your life. The amount of the monthly annuity is calculated by using standardized life expectancy tables, such as the one on p. 21. For example, if you retire when you're 65, your life expectancy is estimated to be another 20 years.

How do you decide which one is best for you? Let's look at each method:

LUMP SUM PAYOUT

Getting your money all at once means you have a tax liability. An alternative is to roll it over into an IRA, invested in any way you choose. Then the lump sum won't be taxed until you take distributions to live on. You could keep it growing, outpacing inflation. Applying the principles you've gleaned from this book, you would want to reinvest the money in comparatively low-risk stocks, bonds, or mutual funds. This is a good strategy if you are comfortable handling your own money, won't be tempted to spend it all at once, or have plenty of other income.

Keep in mind, however, that this is a little riskier than an annuity. First, your investment *could* lose money. Second, should you have unexpected expenses—such as catastrophic, uninsured illness—or other financial difficulties, your retirement money could be drained by creditors.

ANNUITY

An annuity is very safe in that you can't use up your retirement money too quickly or through bad investments. You know exactly how much you will receive each month, so you can budget more easily. As always, though, for such security you pay a price in the form of lower reward. Your monthly payment will not go as far if inflation keeps going its usual way. Also, some annuities are very complicated.

If your retirement fund is large enough to make it worthwhile, you might want to consider taking a portion out in a lump sum and receiving the remainder as an annuity. That way you can take advantage of the best of both systems. But we advise getting an expert's opinion no matter what you finally decide. Know the consequences. The details can be daunting. Fully understanding them can make all the difference in years to come.

Where to Live?

Now that your financial house is in order, it's time to consider your real home. Deciding where you want to live after you retire may be simple: You know that you could never live anywhere but "home," close to your friends and family. Or you decide you will find the location with the lowest cost of living rate of anywhere in the country—or the world—and make your money last even

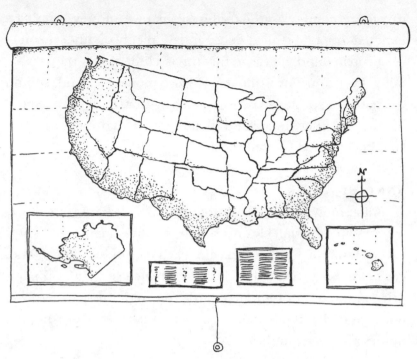

longer. You may have a health condition that means you must live in a certain climate.

Sometimes the decision is more complicated. Perhaps you have three grandchildren on one coast, four on the other, and you live in the Midwest. Where do you retire? Perhaps the cheapest town to live in has no cultural attractions and is too far away from relatives. Or maybe you can't afford to live on your own anywhere, so you must decide which of your children to move in with.

Here are some questions to think about when trying to decide where to live:

- How much will it cost?
- What are the local and state taxes?

- What is the climate like?
- How safe is it?
- How close will I be to my family?
- How close will I be to good medical care?
- Is there recreation or entertainment available?
- Is there good public transportation in case I can't drive anymore?
- Will I have peers or some form of community?
- Is my religious group represented?
- Are there opportunities in case I want to volunteer or work part time?

Once you've considered all these issues, the bottom line is: Where do you *want* to live? What does your heart say? If you have your choice, you might want to vacation in places you are considering for retirement as a trial run. Then try subscribing to the town's local newspaper before making a final decision. You can find out a lot about the political, economic, and cultural atmosphere by reading the newspaper.

A number of resources are available to help you research where to live. They range from books to periodicals. (For a complete list of informative titles and organizations, see the Resources.) A magazine called *Where to Retire* lists the following top 20 retirement locations, based on low cost of living, low crime rate, health care quality, affordable housing, social life, and scenic beauty:

1. Asheville,
   North Carolina
2. Bend, Oregon
3. Myrtle Beach,
   South Carolina
4. Oxford, Mississippi
5. Mount Dora, Florida
6. Hot Springs, Arkansas
7. Las Cruces,
   New Mexico
8. Rockport, Texas
9. Palm Desert,
   California
10. Eugene, Oregon
11. Ocala, Florida
12. Chapel Hill,
    North Carolina
13. Charlottesville,
    Virginia
14. Fairhope, Alaska
15. Pinehurst,
    North Carolina
16. Eufaula, Alabama
17. Sarasota, Florida
18. Whidbey Island,
    Washington
19. Santa Fe, New Mexico
20. Marble Falls, Texas

The Retirement Letter, edited by Peter Dickinson in 1993, has its own top five areas. (It's interesting that only one city made both lists.):

1. Prescott, Arizona (for climate)
2. Mountain Home, Arkansas (for great lifestyle at low cost)
3. Roswell, New Mexico (for comfortable low-cost housing)
4. San Diego, California (for health care)
5. Tie between Newport, Rhode Island, Medford-Ashland, Oregon, and Chapel Hill, North Carolina (for recreation and culture)

Housing Options

The kind of housing you will be most comfortable living in depends on several factors. How much money you have to spend, of course, determines your options. But your basic health is an equally important consideration. If you are completely healthy, mentally alert, and able to live independently, you might decide to stay in your own home. This is the most common housing arrangement for seniors, although it has many variations. Ann Brewer's mother is 89. Ann and her sister check on her every day, but she maintains her own home in Beardstown.

Many of us have helped older relatives stay in their own homes. After Hazel's husband died, her sister asked her to come home and help in the care of their mother, who had Alzheimer's disease.

"I moved in with them in September," recalls Hazel. "Around February my sister went into the hospital, and she died in May. I took care of my mother for as long as I could. That was the first of many experiences I had caring for older relatives. Today, with families spread out and more people having to work, there often isn't anyone to take on that kind of task. I think it fell to me so often because I was a retired nurse."

Those who don't have relatives such as Hazel may hire part-time help to continue living in their own home. Called home care, this arrangement may be less expensive than a nursing home and good for people who still are in pretty good shape. Ruth Huston has a lot of experience with home care from the caregiver's perspective. "For the last 10 years or so," says Ruth, "I have been a caretaker, taking care of older people in their homes throughout the nighttime hours. There are many people who do not need the extensive attention of a nursing home but who are not healthy enough to be at home alone for long periods of time. By looking after these people, I enable them to live in their own homes for as long as possible. One of the women I looked after was 91 when she died; I had been with her for eight years."

Retirement communities are great for people who are independent and want to enjoy the company of their peers. They range in size and cost from luxurious single-family homes in developments with security gates, to small one-bedroom apartments in buildings just for seniors. Safety, convenience, and social opportunities are the main advantages of these arrangements. The disadvantages of retirement communities are that they sometimes have restrictions as to pets, visiting hours for grandchildren, or other rules designed to preserve peace and quiet. Make sure you fully understand what rules you'll be expected to adhere to before you move. Find out whether you're allowed to bring your own furniture, have a patio or a garden. Ask about recreational and social events. Are there courses offered? Is there a library nearby or even on site? How about a church, a laundry, a haircutter, a post office, or a drugstore?

Once your health fails, housing alternatives need to be combined with health care. The typical American solution is the nursing home. Unfortunately, nursing homes are very costly. When

Hazel had to place her mother in a nursing home, she says, it was expensive but "still only a fraction of what it would cost today. She was not there long before she died, but she had sufficient funds to cover her expenses. Long-term care is something for which we either must privately budget or cover with insurance."

If you need to help someone find a nursing home or enter one yourself, there are things you'll want to check. Here is a list of questions to use as a starting point:

1. Does it have a current state operating license?
2. Does it participate in Medicare or Medicaid?
3. Is the director qualified, licensed, and helpful?
4. What is the general feeling when you're in the home? Is it pleasant and cheerful?
5. Do staff members seem upbeat and polite?
6. Do residents seem relatively content and looked after?
7. Have you gotten good recommendations for the home from current residents, relatives, or friends?
8. May residents keep their possessions or wear their own clothes?
9. Are both private rooms and common areas clean and pleasant?
10. Is there adequate lighting, ventilation, and heating?
11. If physical therapy, special diets, or other services are needed, are they provided?
12. Is smoking allowed?
13. In the event of a fire, are there enough exits, sprinklers, smoke alarms, fire extinguishers, evacuation plans, and emergency lighting?
14. Are bathrooms safe, accessible, and designed specially for elderly people?

15. Is there a doctor on call or on staff *at all times*?
16. Is there a registered nurse on duty *at all times*?
17. Can residents call for help easily?
18. Is there a good hospital nearby?
19. Will the home arrange for transportation to the hospital if necessary?
20. Is there an arrangement for dental care?
21. Does the food seem nourishing, plentiful, and appealing?
22. Are there activities offered to residents of varying abilities?
23. Do residents have enough privacy both in their own rooms and in bathrooms?
24. Are visiting hours convenient for everyone concerned?
25. What is the cost? How does it compare to other facilities?

Nursing homes are not the only option, however, even if you become frail or ill. There are new retirement alternatives that are mushrooming around the country. Continuing care retirement communities combine many features in one location. They offer accommodations for every stage of a senior citizen's life, from healthy and independent to needing full-time medical attention. You pay an "entrance fee" as well as a regular service fee for a lifetime guarantee of care and a place to live. Naturally, the entrance fee can be large. The monthly service fee depends on which of the community's facilities you are currently living in.

There are lots of variations on the continuing care theme. For example, a modified continuing care community offers only some health care and therefore charges lower fees. You pay for additional medical care on an as-needed basis. If you have no reason to suspect that you will suffer from illness or need long-term care, you might be better off choosing this less expensive arrangement.

Other alternatives can be created to suit your individual needs. Perhaps you'd be happier sharing a home with a younger roommate, a college student or grandchild. Maybe a motor home parked at your son's or daughter's house would suit you. Or you might want to look into the Elder Cottage Housing Opportunity. Known as ECHO, it provides seniors with apartment-like units to attach to an existing home. They're portable, reusable, and removable. If your grown child prefers not to add a mother-in-law apartment that will be used only a short time, ECHO could be the solution.

Watch Out!

While we don't want to dwell on this section, it does bear mentioning that older people sometimes are victimized. Some financial planners prey on the elderly, knowing that they often are worried about money yet may have some extra cash, that they are isolated and perhaps not as quick to notice a con artist as they once were. It's easy to avoid such unscrupulous salespeople, however. First, don't buy a financial product or make an investment over the phone. (Of course, this does not apply to talking with your own trusted stockbroker over the telephone.) If someone gets you on the phone, follow these hints from the National Fraud Information Center:

1. Don't give out your credit card number, personal identification number, name of your bank, or your checking account number.
2. Ask the person how they got your name, and ask their name, address, and phone number.
3. If you get one of those postcards or a phone call saying you won a prize, ignore it. Too often it's a ploy to get you to buy something before you can claim your "prize."
4. If the person claims to be representing a charity, ask if it's a volunteer or paid position. Ask how much of your donation actually will go to the charity, as opposed to administrative and fund-raising costs.

Next, try to avoid buying financial products from anyone who makes a living based on commissions from such sales. It's better to get advice from a fee-based financial consultant who is selling expertise, not investments. Take it from Hazel, who says, "Having more awareness of money and what it can and cannot do is something I have learned from the club. You can start on a small scale. One thing I know I've done right when I've had to make important financial decisions is seek information from people I trusted." To find a financial planner you can trust, start by asking friends or relatives for suggestions. You also can try calling one of the financial planning organizations listed in the Resource section.

Finally, get a second opinion. If a funeral home director, for example, offers to "let" you prepay your own funeral expenses, you might think that would be a thoughtful gesture for your heirs. But before you sign on the dotted line, it would be wise to check with those heirs, another funeral home, or your lawyer or accountant. It could be a waste of money. The same principle applies to life insurance, limited partnerships, and home improvement scams. Buyer beware: There's no reason to rush into a purchase. If it's a truly legitimate good deal, it will be available the next day, week, or month.

Investment Clubs Revisited

Another possibility for both fun and financial advice support after you've retired is to start an investment club, as we did in Beardstown. Elsie Scheer is a perfect example of a retiree who has been able to make the most of her retirement by joining our club.

"I began to learn after I joined in 1983," Elsie recalls. "I was always afraid of investing because I just didn't trust it. I like to have my money where I can get hold of it right away. I always felt I could get to it if I had it in the bank.

"But they say, even though you have fear, you have to let go to grow. Instead of leaving it all in CDs and savings, I put some in mutual funds and annuities and also ventured into the low-cost investment plan through National Association of Investors Corporation.

"I feel I've really made use of my investment club knowledge. I don't miss my monthly $25. I would probably spend it on something I could not ever account for anyway."

> *We recently traveled to the former Soviet Union as part of a People to People Exchange program. We spent most of our time with folks who, like us, are in agriculture. They have so terribly far to go to catch up with world market agriculture! While very daunting, that is only one of many severe problems. Compared to them, our retirement obstacles are minor.*
>
> **—Carnell Korsmeyer**

If Elsie inspires you to start or find your own investment club, you might want to refer to our first book, *The Beardstown Ladies' Common-Sense Investment Guide,* for more details.

The Good News

The world may not be your oyster, but there are plenty of fish in the sea for retirees. Once you reach a certain age, many companies offer discounts. As baby boomers age and the number of older Americans increases, no doubt we can expect some good bargains. The amount can range from 10 percent off a regular price to nothing in the case of free admission to certain places. Airlines, car rental agencies, hotels, restaurants, clubs, movies, and tour operators all usually have special deals for seniors. Even most state governments provide discounts to state parks and resorts. The age for eligibility differs all the way from a surprisingly young 50 for certain hotel chains, such as Days Inn and Econo-Lodge, to the more standard 62 for most airlines.

Here's a sampling of some of the more worthwhile discounts and deals:

Amtrak Railways. For travel on weekdays, seniors get 15 percent off fares.

Avis Car Rental. Starting at 50 years old, you receive between 5 and 15 percent off.

Choice Hotel International. This company, which owns Quality Inns, Comfort Inns, Clarion Hotels, Calina Quality Inns, and Sleep Inns, offers a minimum of 10 percent off room rates and can go up as high as 30 percent for those 50 years and older.

Continental Airlines. For a one-time fee you can travel anywhere in the country for one year. Also a straight 10 percent discount off all fares is available for anyone 62 and older.

Frisch's Restaurants. This chain has special menus for seniors.

Howard Johnson Hotels. If you're either 61 or an AARP member, you qualify for 15 to 30 percent off room rates. *Scandinavian Airlines.* Although there are no discounts for travel between the United States and Scandinavia, once you get over there, it's 50 percent off travel within Sweden. *State of Colorado.* A $10-pass gives Colorado seniors free admission to state parks and free camping on weekdays. *State of Illinois.* For those 65 and older, there is free hunting and fishing. *TGI Friday's.* These restaurants give seniors half off on all hot drinks such as coffee or tea. *United Airlines.* You can buy a book of four or eight one-way coupons if you're 62 or older.

Remember it rarely hurts to ask. Any time you are spending money, if you are 50 years old or more, inquire about special rates for your age group. Don't be shy—after years of paying full price, you deserve a break!

Finishing Stitch

1. KEEP AN EYE ON YOUR MONEY EVEN AFTER YOU RETIRE.

2. RESEARCH ALL YOUR OPTIONS FOR HOW TO WITHDRAW YOUR MONEY FROM RETIREMENT PLANS.

3. THINK CAREFULLY ABOUT HOW AND WHERE YOU WANT TO LIVE AFTER YOU RETIRE.

4. TAKE ADVANTAGE OF DISCOUNTS FOR SENIORS.

5. ENJOY EVERY MINUTE OF YOUR GOLDEN YEARS! WE SURE ARE.

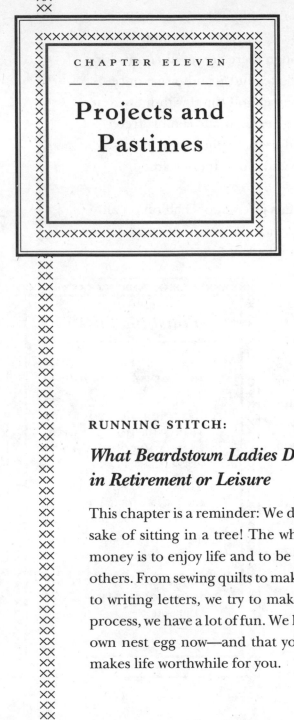

CHAPTER ELEVEN

Projects and Pastimes

RUNNING STITCH:

What Beardstown Ladies Do in Retirement or Leisure

This chapter is a reminder: We don't build our nest eggs for the sake of sitting in a tree! The whole reason for having enough money is to enjoy life and to be able to give something back to others. From sewing quilts to making meals, from collecting glass to writing letters, we try to make the most of our time. In the process, we have a lot of fun. We hope you will start growing your own nest egg now—and that you will make time for whatever makes life worthwhile for you.

Ann Brewer

I graduated from high school at 17 and was employed as board secretary for the Board of Education in Beardstown. I worked a year and then married my high school sweetheart. If my kids had done that I would have killed them! Not too many from our class went on to college, as money was tight. When I began my job back then, I never dreamed I'd be here 45 years later. At the time, I was living for the moment.

In my spare time, I like to read travel articles, movie reviews, three newspapers (two daily and one weekly), novels during vacations, and most important and most faithfully, *Better Investing* magazine. For me, the chance to travel is one of the great benefits following the book. We've made several

Ann Brewer, receiving a certificate from the Illinois State Board of Education.

trips as a group and I enjoyed the trip to Disney World immensely. I like to browse the craft stores and fairs. But I don't devote my time to any particular craft or hobby. We all have much less time than we used to.

Here is a recipe for a salad which doesn't take very long to make. My sister served this salad at her house 25 years ago for some occasion, and my family loved it, so I asked for the recipe. My sister said it was her husband's Aunt Ruby's salad. I remember copying the recipe on the back of a blank check. I still have that original copy and use it when I make the salad. Since it is a

Aunt Ruby's Salad

1 small package lemon gelatin
8 marshmallows (or equivalent using miniatures)
1 small can crushed pineapple
2 large bananas, sliced
¼ cup sugar
1 small egg, beaten
1 teaspoon flour
½ cup whipped cream or substitute
Grated cheddar cheese

Note: I double this recipe for family dinners.

Dissolve gelatin in 1 cup boiling water. Cut up marshmallows (or use miniatures), add to gelatin in a square pan or pie dish and stir until dissolved. Drain canned pineapple and save juice. When gelatin mixture is cool, add pineapple and bananas.

In a saucepan, combine pineapple juice, sugar, beaten egg, and flour. Cook mixture until it thickens. Remove from heat. When cold, add whipped cream or substitute. (I use Cool Whip.) Spread over gelatin mixture and top with grated cheese. Allow to set.

favorite at family gatherings, someone always asks, "Who is going to bring Aunt Ruby's salad?" It is easy to prepare, and young and old alike seem to enjoy it. In other words, you can get the kids to eat it.

Ann Corley

Each year the Heart of Illinois Council, of which we are members, plays a game by investing an imaginary $10,000 in the stock market. The person who has the highest profit in a set time period is the winner. The prize for the first three years was one of Shirley's paintings. Maxine and Lillian tied the second year and both received a painting. I won the third year. Shirley let the winners choose their painting, which wasn't easy because they are all so beautiful. She is a professional. Maxine, Lillian, and I chose paintings of a large leafy tree, each in different colors depicting different seasons.

I became a collector of Depression era glassware almost by accident. One day I was going through some antique books, and I saw pictures of a few dishes I had inherited from my mother. I was real thrilled. I didn't realize what I had was considered that valuable. I was sure surprised to find it listed in a book.

My mother had owned these pieces since she was young. I've learned some of them came as promotions, but she bought others simply because she liked pretty things. Some of the pieces she had were Heritage glass made in the late 1930s by the Federal Glass Company in Ohio.

I became a collector and spent a lot of time studying the different types of glass, the styles and patterns and colors. I also had a pretty good idea of the prices. My son, Larry, and I would go

Ann Corley, back from a day of fishing.

to auctions and shows. I was never concerned too much with their prices and appreciation. I just bought what appealed to me, but Depression glass has skyrocketed in value in recent years.

One of my favorite pieces is a large, gold-colored bowl that I have on display in my home, but you can only keep so many pieces on display. I have the others wrapped safely and stored in boxes. I like to get them out from time to time and look at them, but I never use them because I want to keep them in perfect condition.

Probably the best buy I ever got was an aqua-colored candy dish with a dolphin stem. I've rarely seen one like it. I was on my way home one afternoon, and I saw a sale so I stopped to see what the woman had left. I didn't really like this dish at first, but I felt I should buy something. She said, "If you like it you can have it for a dollar." When I got it home, the more I looked at it the more I liked it.

I don't collect much anymore. But when my sons see a piece they think is pretty, they'll bring it to me as a gift. They know that, like my mother, I enjoy pretty things.

Doris Edwards

In 1959 I became a teaching principal at Washington Elementary School, where I also taught first grade. When my superintendent asked, "How is it going?" my reply was "I can do both jobs for a while, but don't expect me to keep it up too long." Twenty years was quite a while. Then with the budget cuts, I became principal of two buildings in the Beardstown District. Today I am full-time principal at Gard Elementary School.

Just recently I met a former student, someone I had taught in 1942. She exclaimed, "I've read the Beardstown Ladies' book!

Doris, with Jennifer and Jamie, two of her thirty-six great-nieces.

You were one of my favorite teachers and still are." That remark brings to mind the realization of how much teachers touch the lives of their students. There is a great deal of satisfaction in helping others to learn.

How fortunate I was to have good teachers for my formal education. But the best teachers of all were my parents. Our family sat down for all meals together around the dining room table. It was there that the events of the day, both local and global, were discussed.

Whether it be education about finances or any other kind of learning, there is only so much schools can do. Learning must begin in the home. My mother was always drawing our attention to different sights and sounds around us. She would say, "Listen to the redbird sing. Look at the pretty sunset. Did you notice how many walnuts are on the walnut tree? What a beautiful field of wheat." She was teaching us to be observing and curious. These are skills that can be learned and that should be taught from the time a child is old enough to see and hear.

I have a number of hobbies, but my two favorite ones are traveling and enjoying the company of my family. I have 21 nieces and nephews and 36 great-nieces and nephews. I frequently combine traveling with entertaining these young people. Oftentimes one or more of them and sometimes some of their friends have accompanied me on trips. I have been in every state, including Alaska and Hawaii, as well as making several trips to Canada and Europe.

When traveling, we stop and visit historical sites and take pictures. I point out different scenes to my young relatives and friends. Many children today go along with their heads down, oblivious of the world around them. I believe that the world is full of wonder, but one has to look to see it.

Quite a few of the younger members of the family have graduated from high school or college and moved away from Beardstown. To keep in touch with these young people, I write to them the news of the family and the local area.

Although letter writing is said to be becoming a lost art, when I sit down to hand write a letter I usually don't have too much trouble coming up with five or six pages. I try to be concise yet informative. I like to write about my travels and the places I'm planning to visit. I also let my nieces and nephews know what the other family members are doing. I believe that it is important for families to stay close, and informing the young people about each other's lives is helpful in fostering that family closeness. When I get my mail the first thing I do is look to see if there are any personal letters, and I'm sure the people I write to do the same.

As I near retirement, I look with satisfaction on the lives of my young relatives. It is evident that the importance of education and financial stability has been instilled in them. They are heading into a brighter future while providing not only love and guidance, but also opportunities and examples for their children. There is much contentment and pleasure for me knowing that I have played a small part in the success of their lives.

Sylvia Gaushell

I'm proud of my French-Huguenot ancestry. My family has been traced back to France in 1572. I was born in 1911 and raised in Quincy, Illinois. I was an art supervisor in the public schools in Quincy. Once our children started coming I stayed home with them. My daughter Sharon is a part-time secretary in a law firm in Washington, D.C., after working for 34 years as secretary to U.S. Representative Robert Michel (R-Ill.). She raises and shows Sealyham dogs. My son Dennis lives near San Francisco and owns his own computer consulting business.

I've been interested in art all my life and have painted many pictures in oil, acrylic, pastel chalk, and watercolor. I've also done china painting. Although I'm not Catholic, I learned to paint from a nun in a convent in my hometown of Quincy. She had studied in Europe, and I took lessons from her. My son hikes in the Sierras in California and sends me photos. I paint pictures from them.

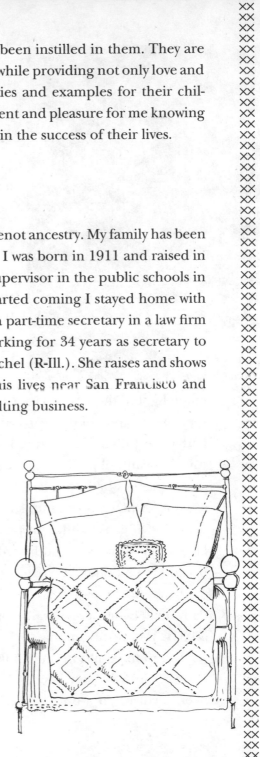

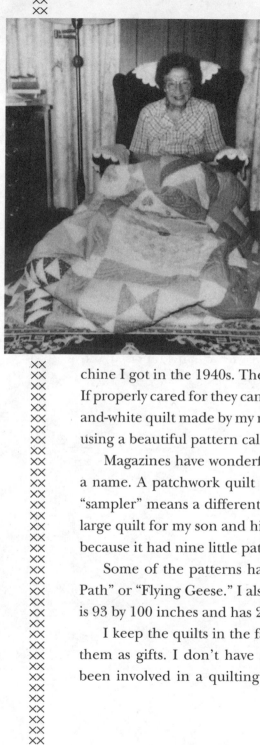

I read many library books on art and cooking. I like to try a new recipe every week. I do crossword puzzles and watch *Jeopardy!* to keep my mind alert. Sometimes I do better than the contestants on the show. I also like television murder mysteries.

In recent years I have sewed six quilts and started two others, all on a portable Singer sewing machine I got in the 1940s. There is nothing like a beautiful quilt. If properly cared for they can last 100 years or more. I have a red-and-white quilt made by my mother's grandmother in the 1880s using a beautiful pattern called "Irish Chain."

Magazines have wonderful quilt patterns. Each pattern has a name. A patchwork quilt is a lot of scraps sewn together. A "sampler" means a different pattern for each square. I made a large quilt for my son and his wife. It was called a "nine-patch," because it had nine little patches in each square.

Some of the patterns have funny names, like "Drunkard's Path" or "Flying Geese." I also made a blue-and-white quilt that is 93 by 100 inches and has 25 large squares.

I keep the quilts in the family, either saving them or giving them as gifts. I don't have any hanging. Although I've never been involved in a quilting bee, I have taken lessons from a woman who had a shop in town for a while. She taught me how to sew the squares together with connecting pieces that form the background pattern. I like to work with cotton because it washes well and doesn't fade. Personally, I like lots of color. I buy the cotton fabric at Wal-Mart or a fabric store.

The back of the quilt is one large piece of plain cotton. It doesn't have to be white. Cotton filler goes in between the face of the quilt and the backing. You can buy it in all different thicknesses.

Never store a quilt in a plastic bag because cotton needs to breathe. It's better to keep it in an old pillow case.

Shirley Gross

Painting is something I always wanted to do but I never seemed to have the time. In the late 1960s, when my two kids were off on their own, I tagged along with a small group that took classes in the nearby town of Jacksonville. I went to observe but the teacher said, "Don't just look," so I made a little, teeny drawing of a still life. I wound up falling in love with painting. The owner of the local art supply store was in the studio that

Shirley, sketching in her backyard.

day. He took me down to the store, and I spent all the money I had right on the spot. I've been with them ever since, and I still go over to Jacksonville to paint once a week. I also have a small studio in my home.

Painting gets me outdoors. I love to paint landscapes, and I never go out when I don't see deer or pheasant or wild turkeys.

I keep a ledger, and every time I finish a painting I write down the date and whether it is in oil or pastels. Later I write what I've done with it, whether I sold it or gave it as a gift. I have dozens of paintings hanging in my home.

When I do sell a painting, I put the money to a good cause. For instance, our church needed to refinish the doors, so I sold some paintings and we were able to get the doors refinished. I am now selling some paintings to help pay for a computer for the church.

If I am having a bad day, I can sit down at the easel and turn everything off. I am trying for the three-dimensional on the two-dimensional. This is the basic challenge of painting: to take three-dimensional images and duplicate them in a two-dimensional art form. You are looking at something two-dimensional but, thanks to the skill of the artist, you see it in three dimensions.

Some people go down to the tavern and bend the elbow all evening. I sit at the easel with my brush. I end up with something, and it's not a hangover.

Margaret Houchins

My husband, Jerry, and I have three businesses. We're real entrepreneurs. I run Countryside Florist on Wall Street in Beardstown and Jerry has a heating and air-conditioning business in

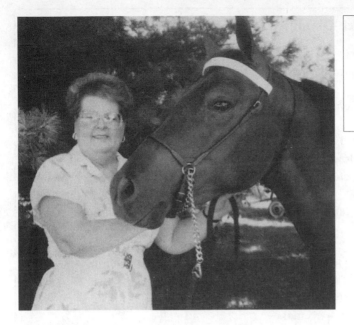

Margaret and her prize-winning horse, Ramble On Miss Target.

the same building right next door. Together, we breed and train horses— Missouri Foxtrotters. In 1994 our horse, Ramble On Miss Target, won the Illinois Breeder's Cup Model Horse, and in 1995 she won the Illinois Championship Fox Trotter Model Horse. Our other horses have won many other ribbons, also. Jerry's horse King Nidon's Pride has won over 60 ribbons in performance classes.

Any day of the week, he'd rather be out "horsing around." He loves it. In the summer, people come to our place and ride and Jerry gives lessons. How profitable a venture this will be for us, only time will tell.

When I look back 10 years, they have gone by so fast, so what is the next 15 years? Nothing. They'll fly by. Jerry and I started saving in the nick of time.

Meanwhile, I like to make dried flower wreaths to sell in my shop and to give as gifts. I learned to make them at the Jean

16-Inch-Diameter Dried Flower Wreath

Foam ring
Small 6-ounce bag Spanish moss
Greening pins
1 florist bunch fresh lemon leaf
   (salal)
1 large head cockscomb (celosia)
3 medium dried sunflower heads
3 dried hydrangea clusters (can be
   tinted with paint)
3 dried pepperberry stems
1 black pipe cleaner

1. Insert two holes 1/2 inch from top front outer edge of foam ring, working front to back. Insert pipe cleaner. Twist to secure. This makes the hanger.
2. Cover front of wreath with Spanish moss, pulling it over sides to back of wreath and securing with greening pins.

3. Dip fresh salal stems into hot glue and then onto wreath to secure. Completely cover front and sides with salal. Do not cover back.
4. Decorate the wreath using a variety of dried flowers. For this wreath I've chosen sunflowers, hydrangeas, and pepperberries. Place flower heads in wreath working in triangle shape. Secure stems by dipping in hot glue before inserting into foam through salal leaf.
5. Be creative and have fun.

Williams School of Design in Springfield, Illinois. You can get the supplies, even the dried flowers, at your local florist or in any good crafts store.

The instructions here are for a multicolored wreath, which is suitable for any room in the home. Sunflowers last forever and are popular these days, especially as a kitchen motif. But the wreath is elegant enough to also hang in a living room. If you use a smaller ring, it would even be lovely in a bathroom. This wreath makes a great wedding or anniversary gift. A new bride would love it.

Ruth Huston

Norman and I used to close our business for the first two weeks of July and take our son Dale on driving vacations across the country. It had been so long since I had traveled, until we went to New York for the *Donahue* show. I was excited because it was my first time in a commercial airplane. As I packed, I couldn't remember the last time I had had my hands inside a suitcase. The thrill of it all is hard to describe.

I was in Jacksonville, a town near Beardstown, recently, and a man I did not know came up to me and said, "You're one of the Beardstown Ladies, aren't you?" That is the kind of thing that leaves me speechless.

I have heard from old friends across the coun-

Ruth in front of her thimble collection, holding one of her China paintings.

try who have seen us on television or read about us in newspapers. My scrapbook is overflowing with pictures, clippings, and mementos from all the places we've been. It's amazing, but it goes to show you that new and different things can happen to you at any age.

For instance, a friend of mine who had lived in Peoria retired and moved back to Beardstown. She had her own kiln and gave classes in china painting. I studied with her and china painting became my favorite hobby.

I've made plates, vases, ashtrays and so forth. It takes several class periods to make a piece. I do not draw free hand on the china. I trace from a picture that suits my taste. I'm partial to roses and pink is my favorite color. I trace over the picture I've selected and use carbon paper to make an image on the china. Then we paint over the image. You must fire the china once for each color you use. I've used six or seven colors on some pieces so it can take a long time to make one piece.

Our teacher supplied everything we needed for the class, the plain, new china, called greenware, and the special paints. You could use the pieces once they are finished, but I never have. Hopefully, they turn out pretty and I wouldn't want to risk something happening to them. I have given away everything except one plate with a pink rose that I have hanging on the wall in my dining room.

I haven't made any new pieces in a few years. We all have much less time for this sort of thing than we used to.

Carnell Korsmeyer

My life as a farmer began when I married one. I did work for a brief time as a dental assistant and office manager when three

Carnell (far left), white-water rafting on the Snake River in Jackson, Wyoming.

of our children were in college and one in high school. But my primary career role has been as the office person for our family pork production business. We built a farm business that marketed 12,000 hogs per year. It required a large investment of energy and resources. These are hard times for many family farmers, but we've been relatively fortunate.

Over the years, the time I might spend on hobbies has been used in voluntary service to persons and organizations. This includes Sunday school teaching, PTA, 4-H leadership, hospital auxiliary, driving cancer patients to treatment, United Way, various committees and boards of the pork industry, etc.

The involvement with the pork industry has led to one interesting hobby of sorts. After we became intensive pork producers in 1968, as opposed to general farmers, somehow I began collecting pigs. Friends and associates saw this as "the" appropriate gift for Carnell! Our collection has grown to dozens, maybe hundreds of pigs of all kinds. They're made of ceramic, cut glass, copper, wood, fabric, you name it.

We have Delft china pig salt and pepper shakers we found in Holland while on vacation. We couldn't resist. Another treasure is a pig made of jade sent to us by a Chinese man who stayed with us for a year as part of an agricultural foreign exchange. When he returned to the U.S. for a visit he brought a pig of Chinese breed made of the same jade—two treasures!

On the front porch we have a large iron pig, which is actually a weathervane. In our dining room there is a wooden pig wearing a chef's hat, and he holds a board on which I write the menu for the day. We have a wall-hanging pig on which is embroidered the message "Never wrestle with a pig. You both get all muddy and the pig likes it."

One of the ceramic pigs was an appreciation gift from an Illinois Pork Industry Queen.

I don't exactly know how we came to have so many. Some we have not been able to resist bringing home, but many were given to us by our children, friends, or people we met through business and activities.

We've had a good life producing pork and as each of these pigs represents a wonderful experience, I'm sure we could collect many, many more.

Helen Kramer

I worked at the bank for 50 years. When I retired they said one thing I had to promise was that I would bring cookies, cake, or a sweet bread on Thursdays. These days the bank has two locations and a drive-in, so I make three stops.

Here is one of my favorite recipes. Amish Friendship Bread begins with a yeast that is passed on from friend to friend and, if properly cared for, can last indefinitely.

In the old days, before commercial yeast was available, pioneer cooks de-

Helen, in the limousine on the way to tape DONAHUE.

pended on these "starters" for their bread making. The recipe calls for beginning with some of the starter passed to you by a friend, but if you don't have one you can make your own. Just mix a package or cake of yeast with two cups flour and two cups water. Use a glass or pottery bowl—never metal of any kind. Cover and let stand at room temperature for 48 hours.

Tend the starter you've either made or received from a friend for 10 days as follows:

Day 1: Do nothing with starter.

Days 2–5: Stir with a wooden spoon.

Day 6: Add 1 cup flour, 1 cup sugar, 1 cup milk, and stir.

Days 7–9: Stir with wooden spoon.

Day 10: Same as Day 6.

Note: The starter will keep for a week in the refrigerator or can be frozen.

Next, follow these instructions to use the starter in the bread.

Amish Friendship Bread

1 cup oil
½ cup milk
3 eggs
1 teaspoon vanilla
2 cups flour
1 cup sugar
1½ teaspoons baking powder
2 teaspoons cinnamon
½ teaspoon salt
½ teaspoon baking soda
1 cup chopped nuts (optional)
1 box instant vanilla pudding

Take out 3 cups starter. Give 1 cup away to each of two good friends and keep the third. With what is left in the bowl, make bread as follows.

To the starter in the bowl, add 1 cup oil, ½ cup milk, 3 eggs, 1 teaspoon vanilla, and mix well.

In a separate bowl, mix 2 cups flour, 1 cup sugar, the baking powder, cinnamon, salt, baking soda, chopped nuts, and instant pudding. Add to wet mixture and stir thoroughly.

Grease 2 large loaf pans and line with greased waxed paper. Pour in dough. Sprinkle sugar and cinnamon on top.

Bake at 325°F. for 1 hour.

Let stand 15 minutes before removing loaves.

Hazel Lindahl

I was born in Beardstown in 1907 and left to go to Chicago where I became a nurse. I met my husband there. He worked in a steel foundry, was older than I, and had been in World War I. We married in 1942 and not long after that came back to this area, living in Smithfield, 30 miles north of Beardstown.

After I returned to Beardstown, two friends from church felt I should have some social activity, so they came over and taught me to play bridge. For a while, I substituted in a game my sister Mildred was involved in. When she passed away, they asked me to join.

In the winter, I am part of a Bible study group at my church, and I love to read. But my favorite hobby is bridge. Now I play with two groups, which gives me the chance to play twice a week. One has eight members and the other four, all women.

Our Friday group of four is very social. We arrive at one-thirty and have dessert before we begin playing. If you saw the recipe I contributed to our first book (it starts with a trip to the frozen foods section of your favorite grocery store), you know what kind of cook I am. I usually serve a frozen dessert, like an ice cream cake roll. My fa-

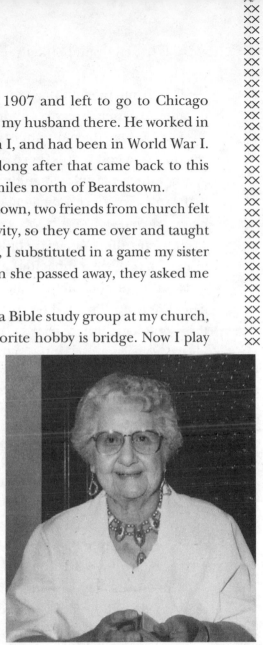

Hazel playing cards, her favorite pastime.

vorite is frozen peanut butter pie. The other ladies usually bake cookies.

Our group of eight plays for money—very high stakes, too: pennies. We usually serve cold drinks and snacks.

I find bridge the most interesting card game I know. Even if you don't get good cards there is always a challenge. Bridge has a wonderful set of rules to guide you. When you play according to the rules, you can legitimately talk across the table to your partner as you bid.

It seems the younger people prefer other card games to bridge, so we have trouble finding substitutes these days. Just as some of my friends helped me learn the game, I helped my neighbor learn. I invited two players over to my house and the three of us taught her. That's how our Friday game got started. It gave her a whole new interest to pursue and that made me feel good. I like doing things for people.

Carol McCombs

My husband, Bill, and I live with our 15-year-old daughter, Cindy, outside Beardstown in a home that adjoins the family farm. My mother, Elsie Scheer, who is a charter member of the investment club, lives next door. On the weekend, with both mowers going, it takes Bill and me five hours to cut our grass and Mom's.

The farm is 240 acres and hasn't been in our family 100 years yet, though I expect we'll reach that mark before long. My brother farms it and lives nearby. Our son, Marty, is 24, and has found his way into farming, too. He manages a hog farm, where he lives with his wife, Jennifer.

I'm a big believer that you can't have a naked goose. I mean a lawn goose, of course. If you are not acquainted with lawn geese, they are yard ornaments and very popular in our neck of the woods. Mine stays on our front porch.

A lawn goose will run you anywhere from $20 up to $50, and you can get them in flower shops or garden supply stores. You an get outfits for your lawn goose in the stores or through craft catalogs, and they'll run you $15 to $30. But I like to make my own. Since you'll want to change the outfits according to the season and on holidays, making the outfits saves a lot of money. Maxine recently purchased a lawn goose, and she lets me dress hers, too.

Carol, on the front porch with her lawn goose.

Here's how to make a great Fourth of July outfit for your goose: Take a half yard of patriotic-looking fabric, seam it up and pin it around the neck of your goose. Now make a hat by cutting a hole in a plastic plate large enough to insert a plastic drink cup. Glue to hold in place. Make two slits on opposite sides of the plate and pass ribbons through the slits. Knot the ribbons at the end to hold them in place. Tie the ribbons beneath the goose's chin. The entire outfit should cost less than $3.

Other tips:

> ❧ *Use bright yellow plastic placemats to make a raincoat and rain hat for inclement weather.*
> ❧ *Fake fur sewed around the neck of a coat made from Christmas-type material makes a great holiday-season outfit.*

Elsie Scheer

My offspring just can't imagine all that Grandma is getting to do. I have 10 grandchildren and seven great-grand-children and the family is growing. When the *20/20* program aired, the camera stopped on a photograph of my oldest daughter's children and grandchildren, a group of 15. My great-grand-son was so thrilled to see his picture on TV, he felt like a star. He took our book to school and read it to his sixth-grade class. Many of us have grand-children and great-grandchildren who have become interested in saving because of our participation in the club. This gives us all terrific satisfaction.

Elsie, preparing a delicious angel food cake in her kitchen.

When we went to the *Donahue* show it was my first time fly-ing. I was not afraid of being on the plane because when your time is up your time is up. My daughter Carol, who is also in the club, was on the plane, and that was a comfort. The most fright-ening thing about flying to me was having to carry my luggage. But of course my friends in the club helped me. Whether old or young, new things can be learned and new experiences are within our reach.

More than 20 years ago I began making corn husk dolls. They make wonderful decorations or centerpieces and are as much fun to give as gifts as they are to make. You don't need very many supplies: just some string, tacky glue, scissors, copper or floral wire, and a needle-nose pliers or wire cutter.

In the fall, when the corn is dry, I go into the fields behind my house and bring in 50 ears at a time. It takes about a dozen corn husks to make one doll. You can buy husks in craft stores, but you don't get near the quality.

When I've got 50 ears or so, I sit and shuck them down. The silks I use for hair. I use the husks to make the dolls' bodies. The husks are almost like parchment. Once you moisten them, they become very pliable and easy to work with. After they dry, they are brittle and hold their shape.

There are many different techniques for making the head, arms, legs, and torso. I use string and wire to tie off different sections of the doll. You also can use husks to make items for the doll to hold, such as flowers, a book, or even a broom. Dyed husks make great clothing such as skirts, or you can use pieces of fabric.

Corn husk dolls can be as simple or elaborate as you care to make them.

Betty Sinnock

I became a teller at the First National Bank of Beardstown in the 1960s and later worked in customer service. In the 1980s, after formation of our investment club, I was pro-

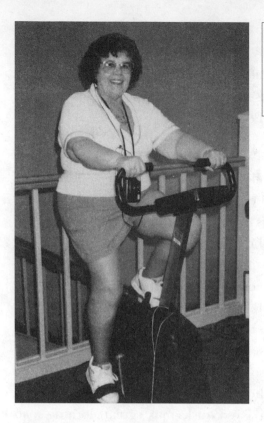

moted to the Trust Department. When the Havana National Bank made me a more attractive offer, I went to work there as a trust officer. I'm very grateful that everyone at the bank has been so supportive of my work with the investment club. We had a huge book signing here with a fabulous cake that looked just like the cover of the book. And they have been very agreeable about giving me time off to go on the publicity tours and other trips. Since the end of the book tours, I've continued to do radio interviews over the phone, usually two to four per day. I've never followed an appointment book so closely in my life.

I don't think I will lack for things to do when I retire. I love to read, especially human interest stories. Bob looks over at me and if the book is sad I've got tears running down my face; if it's happy I'm grinning from ear to ear. I also love gardening, and Bob and I go fishing together.

My pastime, when I find time, is looking for antiques and collectibles. My collecting began with salt and pepper shakers when I was nine or 10 years old. Some were given to me as gifts and some I found when we went on trips. I still have them all packed away. Some I saved in perfect condition and others I let my girls play with when they were young, so who knows what kind of shape they are in.

My first love is early American pattern glass and crystal of all kinds. Like looking for a good stock, I try to find a piece that is affordable and will, when held for a while, increase in value. When Bob and I are on vacation we spend many hours in antique malls and flea markets looking for just the right pieces. Bob is a good hunter and he has found many of our favorite early American pattern glass pieces.

I like beautiful crystal of all types. Aunt Margaret had chosen Fostoria's Dolly Madison pattern crystal and had nearly a complete set of stemware, which I now have. When Bob and I were married in 1952, I chose Clear Caprice pattern by Cambridge Glass Company. We received many pieces for wedding gifts, and through the years we have added to our collection. We not only enjoy looking at our crystal, but I also use it every chance I get. I have been fortunate in that I have broken only a couple of pieces in 43 years.

I also enjoy collecting colored glass vases of all styles. I have 60 or 70 lining the ledge of my glassed-in front porch, creating a rainbow look when the sun shines through.

Collecting has been a satisfying hobby throughout my life and one I look forward to spending more time with once I retire.

Maxine Thomas

I have lived a very rich and full life, especially raising my sons, traveling with my husband, and working in the bank. I have had sadness and physical problems, but through faith and strong Christian belief, I feel that I have done well. Two years ago I began to lose my eyesight. It got so bad my friends in the investment club would have to pick me up for meetings. Specialists said there was nothing to be done. I was going blind. I had thought of buying a new house. But now I wanted to be where things were familiar.

Then I found a doctor who was willing to operate. I had surgeries on both eyes, one month apart, and they worked. I call it a miracle. I see as well as I used to and am back driving myself to meetings.

Traveling was the one thing Roy and I spent our money on. When we were in our 50s, Roy and I began taking a trip every two years. We went to Hawaii. We went to the Caribbean twice, and the second time we went through the Panama Canal. After Roy died, my dear friend Lillian Ellis and I became traveling companions. We often went on educational trips, as chaperones for students. You carry your own luggage, but it's fun and more economical. Our last trip together was to the Holy Land. We finished by taking a camel caravan to the pyramids. I talked her into it and I'm glad because pictures of us on camels are priceless.

Besides traveling, I only have one hobby I can think of and that is volunteering. Since I was so blessed by renewed eyesight, I felt I should use part of my leisure time in helping and serving others. A lot of it is through my church and pastor.

We videotape our services for people who cannot get out to church, and I deliver the tapes to them. I also go with Pastor to

Maxine, riding a camel at the pyramids of Giza, Egypt.

each of the nursing homes once a month. He delivers a little message, and I play the organ or piano. They remember the words to the old hymns and love to sing them.

I'm also part of a group that visits people in the nursing homes who don't have anyone to go and see them. We write letters for them.

Four months out of the year I do a meals-on-wheels route. This is for people who can't come to the senior center for a hot lunch. I usually have a partner with me to run the meals up to the doors.

I enjoy the volunteering because I really like people. My pastor paid me a lovely compliment one time. He said, "Maxine listens with her heart." I've always enjoyed sharing my time. And I hope someone does the same for me someday.

Buffy Tillitt-Pratt

I think of a hobby as something you do when you are not earning a living, which gives you pleasure, which you find relaxing,
and which may, as with embroidery or painting, someday pro-
duce some kind of product.

By that definition, my hobby is motherhood, a hobby sent to
me directly from God. It's the most enjoyable pastime I've ever
had. Can you imagine a hobby that is so absorbing that it takes
nine months just to assemble the "ingredients"? You can't pick
it up or drop it whenever you want, either. It is intense and requires complete dedication.

For the longest time I thought I couldn't have children. I was
40 when T.J. came along, and it was the perfect time. I'm twice
as old as many of the mothers around here. These young moms
are my clients, working hard to buy their first home. It's great
being an older mom because you are financially stable and emotionally secure. You know who you are and that makes you better able to care for this beautiful little being who is so dependent
upon you.

I have been driven all my life. I was driven to succeed in work
and driven to perfectionism. When I had T.J. I thought, "This
will be a little interruption but I'll soon straighten it all out and
get right back to work."

But having him has been the most pleasant interruption in
my driven life. He has slowed me down, and that's exactly what
I needed. I never thought I could just sit and watch this little crea-
ture without thinking, I ought to be out doing this or that. In
the past, if my income had gone down, it would have worried me
terribly. Amazingly, I haven't minded cutting back my work,
which cuts back the amount I can make in a year. T.J. has taught

Buffy and her son T.J. playing at the park.

me that money is nothing in relation to the truly important things in life.

He has even become incorporated into my work life. His first year he was at the office every day, and now he comes with me to show houses in the evenings and on Saturdays. He loves to hold the keys and open the closet doors, and my customers love him.

After work, we like to play. I take him fishing and to watch Daddy drive a four-wheel drive in mud races. He loves to go to McDonald's to play in the ball pit. He could recognize the golden arches and say "Ds" for McDonald's almost before he could say Mommy! Of course, I promptly bought him some of his own stock in McDonald's.

I consider him my greatest hobby because the time I spend with him makes me more relaxed; he gives me so much pleasure.

I look forward to seeing him when we're apart, and I hope I'm creating a beautiful end product: a young man who is strong and confident and who has learned his lessons well.

A Few Last Words

I think our appeal is that we are common, ordinary, working women. A nurse, teachers, bankers, women in business for ourselves. We have learned bit by bit and we have managed to put this together.

We have developed close friendships. One of my favorite articles was by a **New York Times** *writer who came to see us. He wrote that after spending an afternoon with us, it was clear we are having the time of our lives. We are.*

—Shirley Gross

We do hope you've enjoyed reading our book as much as we've enjoyed working on it. If you've learned one or two things about how to save and invest, then we think your money was well spent. But, even more important, if you've picked up a sense of the pure pleasure we get from sharing what we've learned, giving back to others, and just living the best lives we can, then we feel your time was well spent. Maxine likes to keep changing the message on her answering machine. Her favorite, though, the one she seems to record most often, is the following:

"The three things that make life worth living are something to do, someone to love, and something to hope for."

We could not agree more.

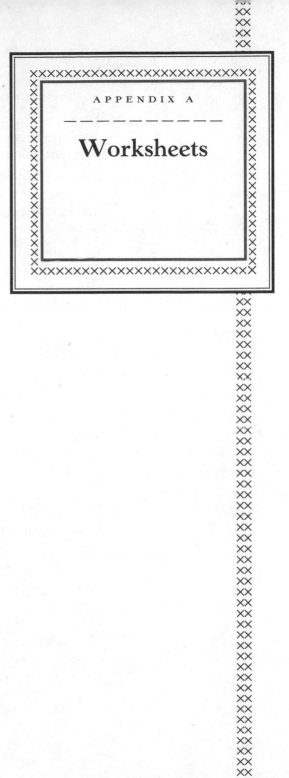

APPENDIX A

Worksheets

RETIREMENT PLANNER

1. $_____.   Enter how much annual income you want to live on in retirement.

2. $_____.   Enter the annual amount you will receive from noninvestment sources, such as Social Security, part-time work, or a pension.

3. $_____.   Subtract Line 2 from Line 1 and enter that amount here. This is the annual income you need to generate in retirement through your investments.

4. $_____.   Enter the amount your nest egg will need to be when you retire to generate the shortfall. Calculate this amount by multiplying Line 3 by your annuity factor. Find your annuity factor in Table A.1. Decide how many years you will be retired and the rate of return you expect on your investment during your retirement.

5. $_____.   Enter your current retirement savings from IRAs, 401(k)s, or any other investment accounts.

6. $_____.   Enter the amount your current savings will be worth when you retire. Calculate this amount by multiplying Line 5 by the savings growth factor in Table A.2.

7. $_____.   Subtract Line 6 from Line 4 and enter that amount here. This is how much more you need to save by the time you retire.

8. $_____.   Enter the amount you need to save annually until you retire to make the amount in Line 7. Calculate this amount by multiplying Line 7 by your annual payment factor. Find your annual payment factor in Table A.3. Decide how many years until you retire and the rate of return you expect on your investments during your working years.

TABLE A-1: ANNUITY FACTOR

Number of
Years You Will
Be in Retirement — *Rate of Return on Investments During Retirement Years*

	4%	6%	8%	10%	12%
20	20.00	16.79	14.31	12.36	10.82
25	25.00	20.08	16.49	13.82	11.80
30	30.00	23.07	18.30	14.93	12.48
35	35.00	25.79	19.79	15.76	12.95
40	40.00	28.26	21.03	16.39	13.28

TABLE A-2: SAVINGS GROWTH FACTOR

Number of Years
Until You Retire — *Rate of Return on Investments Up Until Retirement*

	4%	6%	8%	10%	12%
5	1.00	1.10	1.21	1.32	1.45
10	1.00	1.21	1.46	1.75	2.10
15	1.00	1.33	1.76	2.32	3.04
20	1.00	1.46	2.13	3.07	4.40
25	1.00	1.61	2.57	4.06	6.38
30	1.00	1.77	3.10	5.38	9.24
35	1.00	1.95	3.75	7.12	13.38
40	1.00	2.14	4.52	9.43	19.38

TABLE A-3: ANNUAL PAYMENT FACTOR

Number of Years
Until You Retire — *Rate of Return on Investments Up Until Retirement*

	4%	6%	8%	10%	12%
5	0.200	0.189	0.178	0.168	0.159
10	0.100	0.090	0.081	0.073	0.065
15	0.067	0.057	0.049	0.041	0.035
20	0.050	0.041	0.033	0.026	0.021
25	0.040	0.031	0.024	0.018	0.013
30	0.033	0.024	0.018	0.012	0.009
35	0.029	0.020	0.013	0.009	0.006
40	0.025	0.017	0.011	0.006	0.004

Net Worth Statement (Short)

ASSETS		LIABILITIES	
Checking account	$_____	Mortgage	$_____
Savings account	$_____	Credit card balances	$_____
Money market funds	$_____	Car loans	$_____
Life insurance		Bank loans	$_____
cash values	$_____	School loans	$_____
Stocks/bonds	$_____	Alimony	$_____
Mutual funds	$_____	Other debt	$_____
Certificates of deposit	$_____	Income tax	$_____
IRAs, Keoghs, 401(k)	$_____	Real estate tax	$_____
Pension	$_____	**TOTAL LIABILITIES**	$_____
Real estate (home)	$_____	**TOTAL NET WORTH**	
Real estate (rental,		(Subtract total liabilities	
vacation)	$_____	from total assets)	$_____
Cars	$_____		
Jewelry, art, other			
valuables	$_____		
TOTAL ASSETS	$_____		

Net Worth Statement (Long)

ASSETS	Amount	Date	Taxable, Deductible	Percent Total Portfolio
Cash				
1. Savings accounts	$_____	_____	_____	_____
2. Checking accounts	$_____	_____	_____	_____
3. Money market accounts	$_____	_____	_____	_____
4. Cash value of life insurance	$_____	_____	_____	_____
5. Gold (coins, bullion)	$_____	_____	_____	_____
Fixed Income				
6. CDs	$_____	_____	_____	_____
7. Government securities and funds	$_____	_____	_____	_____
8. Mortgage-backed securities and funds	$_____	_____	_____	_____
9. Corporate bonds and bond funds	$_____	_____	_____	_____
10. Municipal bonds and bond funds	$_____	_____	_____	_____
11. Other fixed-income investments	$_____	_____	_____	_____
Stock				
12. Common stock	$_____	_____	_____	_____
13. Stock mutual funds	$_____	_____	_____	_____
14. Other stock investments	$_____	_____	_____	_____
Real Estate				
15. Land	$_____	_____	_____	_____
16. Income-producing real estate	$_____	_____	_____	_____
17. Real estate limited partnerships	$_____	_____	_____	_____

Net Worth Statement (Long)

ASSETS	Amount	Date	Taxable, Deductible	Percent Total Portfolio
Retirement Accounts				
18. IRAs	$_____	_____	_____	_____
19. 401(k) plans	$_____	_____	_____	_____
20. Keogh or simplified employee pension plan	$_____	_____	_____	_____
21. Vested pension plan	$_____	_____	_____	_____
22. Tax-deferred annuity	$_____	_____	_____	_____
23. Profit-sharing plan	$_____	_____	_____	_____
24. Employee stock-purchase plan	$_____	_____	_____	_____
Personal Assets				
25. Home	$_____	_____	_____	_____
26. Interest in private business	$_____	_____	_____	_____
27. Cars	$_____	_____	_____	_____
28. Jewelry	$_____	_____	_____	_____
29. Valuable collectibles, art, or antiques	$_____	_____	_____	_____
Other				
30. Miscellaneous assets	$_____	_____	_____	_____
TOTAL ASSETS	$_____			

Net Worth Statement (Long)

LIABILITIES	Amount	Date	Taxable, Deductible
1. Mortgage on house	$_____	_____	_____
2. Mortgage on other real estate	$_____	_____	_____
3. Credit cards	$_____	_____	_____
4. Department store charge accounts	$_____	_____	_____
5. Bank loans	$_____	_____	_____
6. Car loans	$_____	_____	_____
7. Home equity loans	$_____	_____	_____
8. Student loans	$_____	_____	_____
9. Income tax	$_____	_____	_____
10. Other tax debts	$_____	_____	_____
11. Broker's margin loans	$_____	_____	_____
12. Miscellaneous other debt	$_____	_____	_____

TOTAL LIABILITIES $_____

NET WORTH
(Total assets minus total liabilities) $_____

Monthly Budget Worksheet #1

INCOME

Take-home paycheck (salary after taxes and any other deductions)	$_____
Second paycheck (if married)	$_____
Any other income	$_____
TOTAL INCOME	$_____

FIXED EXPENSES

Savings and investments	$_____
Mortgage/rent	$_____
Property tax	$_____
Homeowner's insurance	$_____
Life insurance	$_____
Health insurance	$_____
Bank loans	$_____
Car payments	$_____
Car insurance	$_____

OTHER EXPENSES

Groceries	$_____
Clothing	$_____
Medical	$_____
Dental	$_____
Telephone	$_____
Gas/electricity	$_____
Water	$_____
Entertainment	$_____
Gasoline	$_____
Household maintenance	$_____
School supplies, tuition, field trips	$_____
Subscriptions	$_____
Credit card accounts	$_____
Dept. store accounts	$_____
Car maintenance	$_____
Vacation	$_____
Gifts	$_____
Sundries (newspaper, candy, personal care)	$_____
TOTAL EXPENSES	$_____

Monthly Budget Worksheet #2

	Last month	This month (planned)	This month (actual)
INCOME			
Take-home salary	$_____	$_____	$_____
Second take-home salary	$_____	$_____	$_____
Rental income	$_____	$_____	$_____
Interest	$_____	$_____	$_____
Dividends	$_____	$_____	$_____
Trusts	$_____	$_____	$_____
Other business income	$_____	$_____	$_____
Pension	$_____	$_____	$_____
Social Security	$_____	$_____	$_____
Gifts	$_____	$_____	$_____
TOTAL	$_____	$_____	$_____
FIXED EXPENSES			
Savings	$_____	$_____	$_____
Emergency fund	$_____	$_____	$_____
IRAs, Keoghs, or other retirement accounts	$_____	$_____	$_____
Investments	$_____	$_____	$_____
Mortgage or rent	$_____	$_____	$_____
Property tax	$_____	$_____	$_____
Property insurance	$_____	$_____	$_____
Car insurance	$_____	$_____	$_____
Car payments	$_____	$_____	$_____
Health insurance	$_____	$_____	$_____
Life insurance	$_____	$_____	$_____
Home insurance	$_____	$_____	$_____
Bank loans	$_____	$_____	$_____

School loan	$_____	$_____	$_____
Tuition	$_____	$_____	$_____
Child care	$_____	$_____	$_____
1/12 of other yearly expense	$_____	$_____	$_____
TOTAL	$_____	$_____	$_____

NONFIXED EXPENSES

Food	$_____	$_____	$_____
Clothing	$_____	$_____	$_____
Entertainment	$_____	$_____	$_____
Telephone	$_____	$_____	$_____
Electric/gas	$_____	$_____	$_____
Water	$_____	$_____	$_____
Medical	$_____	$_____	$_____
Dental	$_____	$_____	$_____
Veterinarian	$_____	$_____	$_____
Gasoline	$_____	$_____	$_____
Car maintenance (tune-ups, new tires)	$_____	$_____	$_____
Commuting costs (bus, train)	$_____	$_____	$_____
Restaurants	$_____	$_____	$_____
Books, magazines, newspapers	$_____	$_____	$_____
Personal (haircuts, dry cleaner)	$_____	$_____	$_____
Vacation	$_____	$_____	$_____
Gifts	$_____	$_____	$_____
Charitable contributions	$_____	$_____	$_____
TOTAL	$_____	$_____	$_____

Estate Planner

_____

     (name)

Key Names and Phone Numbers

NAME	PHONE NUMBER
Close relatives _____	_____
Attorney _____	_____
Employer _____	_____
Accountant _____	_____
Insurance agents _____	_____
Financial planner _____	_____
Broker _____	_____
Doctors _____	_____
Dentist _____	_____

Key Documents

ESTATE PAPERS	LOCATION
Will _____	_____
Power of attorney _____	_____
Living will _____	_____
Letters of instruction _____	_____
List of financial assets _____	_____

PERSONAL PAPERS   LOCATION

Birth certificate _____ _____

Marriage certificate _____ _____

Social Security card _____ _____

Military records _____ _____

Passport _____ _____

Adoption papers _____ _____

Memberships _____ _____

Subscriptions _____ _____

FINANCIAL ASSETS	**LOCATION**	**ACCOUNT NUMBER**
Pension		
Checking accounts		
Savings accounts		
Credit cards		
CDs		
Stock certificates		
Mutual fund shares		
Bonds		
Savings bonds		
IRAs		
Keogh plans		
401(k) plans		
Annuities		
Stock option plans		

REAL ESTATE   **LOCATION**

Title _____   _____

Deed _____   _____

Mortgage statement _____   _____

Car _____   _____

INSURANCE   **LOCATION**

Life _____   _____

Homeowner's _____   _____

Property _____   _____

Liability _____   _____

Health _____   _____

Dental _____   _____

Disability _____   _____

Car _____   _____

MISCELLANEOUS ITEMS   **LOCATION**

Safety deposit box _____   _____

Income tax return _____   _____

Other _____   _____

INSURANCE PLANNER

1. $_____. Enter the amount of immediate expenses your policy would need to cover, including funeral costs, estate taxes, mortgage, college tuition, and any other debts.

2. $_____. Enter your current household expenses.

3. $_____. Enter how much less Line 2 would be minus your costs for food, clothes, commuting, etc.

4. $_____. Enter how much income your survivors would receive from Social Security benefits, spouse's income, pension, etc.

5. $_____. Enter the amount your family needs to make up in annual income by subtracting Line 4 from Line 3.

6. $_____. Enter your family's living expenses by multiplying Line 5 by the number of years you want your insurance to cover them.

7. $_____. Enter your family's total expenses by adding Line 2 and Line 6.

8. $_____. Enter the cash value of your investments and any lump-sum payments payable upon your death.

9. $_____. Enter your *total necessary insurance coverage* by subtracting Line 8 from Line 7.

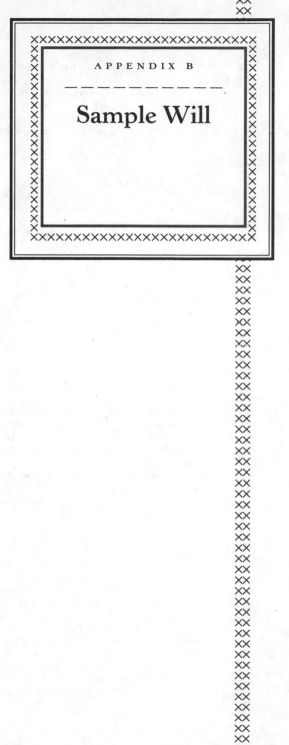

APPENDIX B

Sample Will

WILL

LAST WILL AND TESTAMENT OF_____

     I,_____, currently residing at _____, being of sound and disposing mind, memory and understanding, do hereby declare the following to be my Last Will and Testament, hereby revoking any and all former Wills and Codicils by me heretofore at any time.

     FIRST: I direct that my executor, hereinafter named, pay all of my just debts, funeral expenses and expense of administration of my estate as soon as may be practicable.

     SECOND: I give devise and bequeath all my right, title, and interest to such real property used by me as a place of residence, which I may own at the time of my death, together with the buildings and improvements thereon and the appurtenances thereto, and all china, silverware, furniture, furnishing and other articles of household equipment, books and pictures situated in or about said real property, and all my right, title and interest in and to any and all policies of insurance relating to such property, subject to all mortgages and liens affecting the same, to my wife _____, absolutely, if she shall survive me.

     THIRD: (A) I give and bequeath to my wife, _____, absolutely, if she shall survive me, all the rest of my tangible property, including but not limited to personal effects, jewelry, china, silverware, clothing, furniture, furnishings, and other articles of household equipment, books, pictures, and automobiles; but if she shall not survive me, I give, devise and bequeath said property to my children in as nearly equal shares as possible, as they shall select with the assistance of my Executor, having due regard for their personal preferences, or if only one of them shall survive me, all to the survivor.

     (B) I give, devise and bequeath the rest and residue of my estate (my "residuary estate"), whether real or personal property, tangible or intangible property, wherever located, to my wife, _____.

     FOURTH: If my wife, _____, predeceases me, I give, devise and bequeath the rest and residue of my property which shall be divided in equal shares according to the number of my children surviving me so that there is one trust for each child, to my Trustee, in trust, to hold, manage, invest and reinvest the same, to collect and receive the income therefrom and until each child for whom a trust is established shall attain the age of twenty-two (22) years of age, to pay or apply the net income therefrom at least semiannually, and to invade the trust and pay or apply so much or all of the principal thereof, to or for the use of each of my children in such amounts and proportions as my Trustee in his discretion shall from time to time determine, or to accumulate same. In paying or applying such principal or income, my Trustee in his discretion shall take into consideration the best interests and welfare of my children. Upon each child then living attaining the age of twenty-two (22) years of age, I give, devise and bequeath the principal of such trust, or my residuary estate, as the case may be, to such children then living, *per stirpes*.

     FIFTH: Notwithstanding anything herein to the contrary, in the event any beneficiary hereunder and I shall die at the same time, or as a result of a common accident or catastrophe, or under circumstances such as render it difficult or impossible to determine which of us shall have been the first to die, I direct that I shall be deemed to have survived, and that this my Will shall be so construed.

     SIXTH: I hereby nominate, constitute and appoint my wife, _____, Executrix of this my Will. In the event she shall predecease me, or shall fail to qualify, or, having qualified, shall die, resign or cease to act for any reason as

Executrix, I hereby nominate, constitute and appoint my brother and his wife, and _____, residing in _____, to be Co-Executors of this my Will in her place and stead with all the powers and duties herein granted.

I hereby nominate, constitute, and appoint _____, residing at _____, my Trustee of the Trust for my children under Article "Fourth" of this my Last Will and Testament.

I direct that no bond or other security shall be required of any Executor or Trustee herein named for the faithful performance of his duties as Executor or Trustee with respect to the administration of my estate or any trust hereunder, nor with respect to any advance payment of commissions, in any jurisdiction. All the duties and powers, discretionary and otherwise, imposed or conferred upon my Executor an trustee shall devolve upon their successors.

SEVENTH: If my wife, _____, shall not survive me, I hereby nominate, constitute and appoint my brother-in-law and his wife, _____ and _____, presently residing in _____ to be the guardians of the person and property of my minor children surviving, me, and I direct that no bond or other security shall be required of any such guardian in any jurisdiction. If _____ and predecease me and my wife, or both die while they are guardians of my minor children, then I hereby nominate, constitute and appoint my sister-in-law and her husband, _____ and _____, presently residing in _____, as substitute guardians of the person and property of my minor children surviving me.

EIGHTH: In addition to such powers as they may have by law, except as modified by the following powers, I fully authorize and empower my Executor with respect to any and all property, real, personal or mixed, which may at any time constitute part of my estate, in his sole discretion and without applying to any property at any time held in trust hereunder, whether as principal or income, and until final distribution thereof, in his sole discretion and without applying to any court for permission so to do or for instructions in regard thereto, to retain such property for so long as they may deem advisable, whether or not authorized by law for the investment of trust funds and regardless of any rule as to diversity of trust investments; to borrow money from any person or corporation, including my Executor, and to pledge or mortgage such property as security therefore to employ attorneys, investment counsel and accountants or other agents and to open and maintain a custodian account and in investment counsel account or accounts and to pay their fees from principal or income; to hold property in the name of a nominee or in such form that title thereto may pass by delivery; to treat as income any and all cash dividends, whether ordinary or extraordinary, except liquidating dividends, warrants, rights and similar incidents of stock ownership; to carry out any direction or authorization to pay over income or principal to any beneficiary by applying the same for the benefit of such beneficiary; and, generally, to do all such acts and take all such proceedings with respect to such property as if the absolute owner thereof, and no person dealing with my said Executor shall be obligated to see to the proper applications of any monies paid or delivered.

IN WITNESS WHEREOF, I have hereunto signed my name and affixed my seal to this my Last Will and Testament this 20th day of March, One Thousand Nine Hundred and Ninety-Two.

Resources We Recommend

Organizations

FINANCIAL PLANNING

American Financial Services Association
919 18th Street, NW
Washington, DC 20006
800-727-7389
An organization primarily for those in the business of lending, but provides information to consumers on money management and credit.

American Institute of Certified Public Accountants
1211 Avenue of the Americas
New York, NY 10036
212-596-6200
For referrals on which accountants have earned the designation Accredited Personal Finance Specialists.

Institute of Certified Financial Planners
10065 East Harvard Avenue
Denver, CO 80231
800-282-7526
To find financial planners who charge a fee rather than sell investment products.

International Association for Financial Planning
Two Concourse Parkway, Suite 800
Atlanta, GA 30328
404-395-1605
A general organization of financial planners.

International Society for Retirement Planning
11312 Old Clu Road
Rockville, MD 20852
800-327-4777
For preretirement materials and presentations on retirement topics.

National Association of Investors Corporation
711 West Thirteen-Mile Road
Madison Heights, MI 48071
810-583-6242
For a multitude of resources, especially how to start an investment club.

National Association of Personal Financial Advisors
1130 Lake Cook Road
Buffalo Grove, IL 60089
800-366-2732
A general organization of financial planners.

Pension Rights Center
1918 16th Street
Washington, DC 20006
202-296-3776
For many free publications on pensions.

Social Security Administration Office of Public Inquiries
6401 Security Boulevard
Baltimore, MD 21235
301-594-1234
800-772-1213

For general information and forms.

HEALTH/INSURANCE ISSUES

American Council of Life Insurance
1001 Pennsylvania Avenue NW
Washington, DC 20004
202-624-2000
For publications about life and other insurance.

American Health Care Association
1201 L Street NW
Washington, DC 20005
202-842-4444
For education materials on long-term care.

American Society of Chartered Life Underwriters and Chartered Financial Consultants
270 South Bryn Mawr Avenue
Bryn Mawr, PA 19010
800-392-6900
Chartered financial consultants focusing on all aspects of financial planning.

Health Insurance Association of America
555 13th Street NW
Suite 600E
Washington, DC 20004
202-824-1600
For free publications on long-term care insurance.

National Insurance Consumer Organization
121 North Payne Street
Alexandria, Virginia 22314
800-336-6423
For information on life insurance.

United Seniors Health Cooperative
1334 G Street NW
Washington, DC 20005
202-393-6222
For publications, to have your Medigap insurance checked for adequate coverage.

RETIREMENT LIFESTYLES

Action for Older Persons
144 Washington Street
Binghamton, NY 13901
607-722-1251
Runs a preretirement education program.

American Association of Homes for the Aging
901 E Street NW
Suite 500
Washington, DC 20004
202-296-5960
For information and publications on retirement housing.

American Association of Retired Persons (AARP)
1909 K Street NW
Washington, DC 20049
202-434-2277
For every possible kind of information and publication, from free booklets on housing to a mutual fund to legal advice. If you're a senior American, you should join.

American Society on Aging
833 Market Street
San Francisco, CA 94103
415-974-9600
As part of its many functions, serves as a clearinghouse for information on retirement and aging.

Elderhostel, Inc.
75 Federal Street
Boston, MA 02110
617-426-7788
A network of more than 1,500 cultural and educational institutions around the world that offer short-term, low-cost residential programs for seniors.

Families U.S.A. Foundation
1334 G Street NW
Washington, DC 20005
202-628-3030
For publications on aging.

Gray Panthers
2025 Pennsylvania Avenue NW
Washington, DC 20006
202-466-3132
Its local chapters organize
groups of older and younger
people to advocate for better
housing, transportation, health
care, and other issues in the
community.

**National Association for
Home Care**
519 C Street NE
Washington, DC 20002
202-547-7424
For publications, education,
and standards on home care
workers.

**National Association of Area
Agencies on Aging**
1112 16th Street NW
Washington, DC 20036
202-296-8130
For information and referrals
on aging services.

**National Council on the
Aging**
West Wing 100
600 Maryland Avenue SW
Washington, DC 20024
202-479-1200
An umbrella organization that
includes the National Institute
on Age, Work and Retirement;
National Institute of Financial
Issues and Services for Elders;

National Institute on Adult
Daycare; National Institute of
Senior Centers; and others.

**National Council of Senior
Citizens**
1331 F Street NW
Washington, DC 20004
202-347-8800
An advocacy group for seniors;
publishes the monthly *Senior
Citizen News.*

**National Senior Sports
Association**
PO Box 882
Fairfax, VA 22030
800-282-6772
For information on sports
programs for seniors.

Older Women's League
666 11 Street NW
Washington, DC 20001
202-783-6686
Advocacy group with local
chapters, focusing on women as
they age.

**Service Corps of Retired
Executives**
409 3 Street SW
Washington, DC 20024
If you'd like to share your
business expertise with those
just starting out.

Shared Housing Resource Center

6344 Greene St.
Philadelphia, PA 19144
215-848-1220
Provides information and help on planning and developing group residence programs.

Legal Issues

Legal Counsel for the Elderly

601 E Street NW
Washington, DC 20049
202-434-2120
For general legal advice.

National Academy of Elder Law Attorneys

655 N. Elvernon Way
Tucson, AZ 85711
602-881-4005
For referrals to lawyers specializing in elder law issues.

National Senior Citizens Law Center

2025 M Street NW
Washington, DC 20036
202-887-5280
For help on Social Security and other legal issues.

Books

FINANCIAL PLANNING

Lewis and Karen Caplan Altfest. *Lew Altfest Answers Almost All Your Questions About Money.* New York: McGraw-Hill, 1994.

Alexandra Armstrong and Mary Donahue. *On Your Own: A Widow's Passage to Emotional and Financial Well-Being.* Chicago: Dearborn Financial Publishing, 1993.

Janet Bamford, Jeff Blyskal, Emily Card, and Aileen Jacobson. *The Consumer Reports Money Book: How to Get It, Save It, and Spend It Wisely,* revised edition. Yonkers, NY: Consumer Reports Books, 1992.

The Beardstown Ladies' Investment Club with Leslie Whitaker. *The Beardstown Ladies' Common-Sense Investment Guide.* New York: Hyperion, 1994.

Adriane Berg. *Making Up for Lost Time: Speed Investing for a Secure Future.* New York: Hearst Books, 1994.

Lynn Brenner. *Building Your Nest Egg With Your 401k.* Washington Depot: Investors Press, 1995.

Jane Bryant Quinn. *Making the Most of Your Money.* New York: Simon & Schuster, 1991.

Armond Budish. *Avoiding the Medicaid Trap.* New York:

Henry Holt, 1990.

Ken and Daria Dolan. *The Smart Money Financial Planner*. New York: Berkley Books, 1992.

Robert K. Gardiner. *Dean Witter Guide to Personal Investing*. New York: Signet, 1989.

Charles J. Givens. *Financial Self-Defense: How to Win the Fight for Financial Freedom*. New York: Simon & Schuster, 1990.

Jordan Goodman and Sonny Bloch. *Everyone's Money Book*. Chicago: Dearborn Financial Publishing, 1993.

Hartley Gorden with Jane Daniel. *Remarriage Without Financial Risk*. Financial Planning Institute, 1992.

Robert Hagstrom. *The Warren Buffett Way: Investment Strategies of the World's Greatest Investor*. New York: John Wiley & Sons, 1994.

Daniel Kehrer. *Kiplinger's 12 Steps to a Worry-Free Retirement*. Washington, DC: Kiplinger Books, 1993.

Frances Leonard. *Women & Money: The Independent Woman's Guide to Financial Security for Life*. Redding, MA: Addison-Wesley Publishing, 1991.

Kathryn Maxwell and Steven Sisgold. *Richer Than You Dreamed: How to Take Control of Your Two-Income Family's Finances*. New York: Clarkson N. Potter, 1992.

Jonathan Pond. *The New Century Family Money Book*. New York: Dell, 1993.

Terry Savage. *Terry Savage's New Money Strategies for the '90s*. New York: HarperBusiness, 1993.

Mark Skousen. *Scrooge Investing: The Bargain Hunter's Guide to Discounts, Free Services, Special Privileges & 90 Other Money Saving Tips*. Chicago: Dearborn Financial Publishing, 1994.

James Stowers with Jack Jonathan. *Yes, You Can . . . Achieve Financial Independence*. Kansas City, MO: Deer Publishing, 1992.

Shelby White. *What Every Woman Should Know About Her Husband's Money*. New York: Random House, 1992.

HEALTH/INSURANCE ISSUES

Joseph Matthews. *Elder Care: Choosing and Financing Long-Term Care*. Berkeley, CA: Nolo Press, 1992.

RETIREMENT LIFESTYLES

Richard Boyer and David Savageau. *Retirement Places Rated.* Englewood Cliffs, NJ: Prentice-Hall, 1990.

Linda Bowman. *Freebies (& More) for Folks Over Fifty.* Chicago: Probus Publishing, 1991.

David Brown. *The Rest of Your Life Is the Best of Your Life.* New York: Barricade Books, 1991.

Vivian F. Carlin and Ruth Mansberg, *If I Live to Be 100: A Creative Housing Solution for Older People.* Pennington, NJ: Princeton Book Company, 1989.

Diana Cort-Van Arsdale and Phyllis Newman. *Transitions: A Woman's Guide to Successful Retirement.* New York: HarperCollins, 1992.

Wilbur Cross. *The Henry Holt Retirement Sourcebook.* New York: Henry Holt, 1992.

Hugh Downs. *Fifty to Forever.* Nashville, TN: Thomas Nelson, 1995.

Joan Rattner Heilman. *Unbelievably Good Deals and Great Adventures That You Absolutely Can't Get Unless You're Over 50.* Chicago: Contemporary Books, 1994.

Alice Lee. *A Field Guide to Retirement: 14 Lifestyle Opportunities and Options for a Successful Retirement.* New York: Doubleday, 1991.

Fred and Alice Lee. *The Fifty Best Retirement Communities in America.* New York: St. Martin's Press, 1994.

G. Scott Thomas. *The Rating Guide to Life in America's Small Cities.* Buffalo, NY: Prometheus Books, 1990.

Gordon K. Williamson. *Sooner Than You Think: Mapping a Course for Comfortable Retirement.* Burr Ridge, IL: Irwin Professional Publishing, 1993.

Magazines and Newsletters

FINANCIAL ISSUES

Bottom Line/Tomorrow
Boardroom Publishing
55 Railroad Avenue
Greenwich, CT 06836
203-625-5900

Business Week
McGraw-Hill
1221 Avenue of the Americas, 36th Floor
New York, NY 10020-1095
212-512-6421

Debt-Free and Prosperous Living
MarketLine
824 South Main Street
Crystal Lake, IL 60014
815-356-8800

Forbes
Forbes Publishing
60 Fifth Avenue
New York, NY 10011-8882
212-620-2200

Fortune
Time, Inc.
1271 Avenue of the Americas
Rockefeller Center
New York, NY 10020-1300
212-522-1212

Kiplinger's Personal Finance and
Kiplinger's Retirement Report
Kiplinger Washington Editors,
Inc.
1729 H Street NW
Washington, DC 20006-3924
202-887-6400

Money
Time, Inc.
1271 Avenue of the Americas
Rockefeller Center
New York, NY 10020-1300
212-586-1212

Moody's
Moody's Investors Service, Inc.
99 Church Street
New York, NY 10007-2787
212-553-0300

No-Load Investor
No-Load Fund Investor
PO Box 283

Hastings-on-Hudson, NY 10706
800-252-2042

The Retirement Letter
Phillips Publishing Inc.
7811 Montrose Road
Potomac, MD 20854
301-424-3700

Smart Money
Hearst Corp. & Dow Jones
1790 Broadway
New York, NY 10019
800-444-4204

Standard & Poor's Stock Guide
Standard & Poor's Corp.
25 Broadway
New York, NY 10004
212-208-8000

*Sylvia Porter's Active Retirement
Newsletter*
Sylvia Porter Organization
15 Columbus Circle
New York, NY 10023
212-373-7745

Value Line Investment Survey
Value Line Inc.
220 E. 42nd Street
New York, NY 10017-5891
212-687-3965

Worth
575 Lexington Avenue
New York, NY 10022
212-751-4550

HEALTH AND LIFESTYLE ISSUES

Hot Flash
National Action Forum Midlife & Older Women
PO Box 816
Stony Brook, NY 11790
Health and social issues for women.

Mature Market Report
Lifestyle Change Communications
5885 Glenridge Drive
Atlanta, GA 30328
404-252-0554
Case studies, how-tos, and investigative reports of interest to seniors.

Mature Traveler
GEM Publishing Group
PO Box 50820
Reno, NV 89513
702-786-7419
Deals, trips, and tips for those over 50.

New Choices: For the Best Years
28 W. 23rd Street
New York, NY 10010
212-366-8800

Prime of Life
Kelly Communications
Route 13, Box 28
Charlottesville, VA 22901
804-296-5676
A newsletter of health advice for people over 55.

INTERNAL REVENUE SERVICE PUBLICATIONS

#	Title
1	"Your Rights as a Taxpayer"
17	"Your Federal Income Tax"
54	"Tax Guide for U.S. Citizens and Resident Aliens Abroad"

448	"Federal Estate and Gift Taxes"
463	"Travel, Entertainment, and Gift Expenses"
501	"Exemptions, Standard Deduction, and Filing Information"
502	"Medical and Dental Expenses"
503	"Child and Dependent Care Credit"
504	"Tax Information for Divorced or Separated Individuals"
505	"Tax Withholding and Estimated Tax"
508	"Educational Expenses"
510	"Excise Taxes"
514	"Foreign Tax Credit for Individuals"
516	"Tax Information for U.S. Government Civilian Employees Stationed Abroad"
520	"Scholarships and Fellowships"
521	"Moving Expenses"
523	"Tax Information on Selling Your Home"
524	"Credit for the Elderly or the Disabled"
525	"Taxable and Nontaxable Income"
526	"Charitable Contributions"
527	"Residential Rental Property"
529	"Miscellaneous Deductions"
530	"Tax Information for Homeowners (including Owners of Condominiums and Cooperative Apartments"
533	"Self-Employment Tax"
534	"Depreciation"
535	"Business Expenses"
536	"Net Operating Losses"
537	"Installment Sales"
538	"Accounting Periods and Methods"
539	"Employment Taxes"
541	"Tax Information on Partnerships"
544	"Sales and Other Dispositions of Assets"
547	"Nonbusiness Disasters, Casualties, and Thefts"
550	"Investment Income and Expenses"
551	"Basis of Assets"
552	"Record keeping for Individuals and a List of Tax Publications"
554	"Tax Information for Older Americans"
555	"Community Property and the Federal Income Tax"

556   "Examination of Returns, Appeal Rights, and Claims for Refund"

559   "Tax Information for Survivors, Executors and Administrators"

560   "Retirement Plans for the Self-Employed"

561   "Determining the Value of Donated Property"

564   "Tax Information for Older Americans"

570   "Tax Guide for Individuals in U.S. Possessions"

575   "Pension and Annuity Income"

584   "Nonbusiness Disaster, Casualty, and Theft Loss Workbook"

586A   "The Collection Process (Income Tax Accounts)"

587   "Business of Your Home"

589   "Tax Information on S Corporations"

590   "Individual Retirement Accounts (IRAs)"

593   "Tax Highlights for U.S. Citizens and Residents Going Abroad"

594   "The Collection Process (Employment Tax Accounts)"

596   "Earned Income Credit"

721   "Tax Guide to U.S. Civil Service Retirement Benefits"

901   "U.S. Tax Treaties"

904   "Interrelated Computations for Estate and Gift Taxes"

907   "Tax Information for Handicapped and Disabled Individuals"

908   "Bankruptcy and other Debt Cancellations"

909   "Alternative Minimum Tax for Individuals"

910   "Guide to Free Tax Services"

911   "Tax Information for Direct Sellers"

915   "Social Security Benefits and Equivalent Railroad Retirement Benefits"

916   "Information Returns"

917   "Business Use of a Car"

919   "Is My Withholding Correct?"

924   "Reporting of Real Estate Transactions to IRS"

925   "Passive Activity and At-Risk Rules"

926   "Employment Taxes for Household Employers"

927   "Tax Obligations of Legalized Aliens"

929   "Tax Rules for Children and Dependents"

934   "Supplemental Medicare Premium"

936   "Limits on Home Mortgage Interest Deduction"

1004   "Identification Numbers Under ERISA"

1048   "Filing Requirements for Employee Benefit Plans"

1212   "List of Original Issue Discount Instruments

TELEPHONE HOT LINES

Eldercare Locator 800-677-1116
For referrals to local agencies on elder care.

Institute of Certified Financial Planners 800-282-7526
To find financial planners who charge a fee rather than sell
investment products.

Insurance industry no-fee hot line 800-942-4242
For information and questions about insurance policies.

InsuranceQuote 800-972-1104
SelectQuote 800-343-1985
For free recommendations on low-cost term life insurance.

Office of the Inspector General of the Department of Health and
Human Service 800-368-5779
For Medicare fraud.

Senior Helpline 800-328-7576
More than 100 taped messages on a range of subjects.

U.S. Savings Bonds 800-872-6637
For current savings bonds rates.

Videos

"Aging: Beyond Retirement," Perennial Education, Inc. Call 800-323-
9084 or fax 708-328-6706 to order. Discusses the need to continue
activity after retirement.

Cookin' Up Profits on Wall Street, The Beardstown Ladies. Call 800-359-
3276 to order or use the coupon at the end of this book.

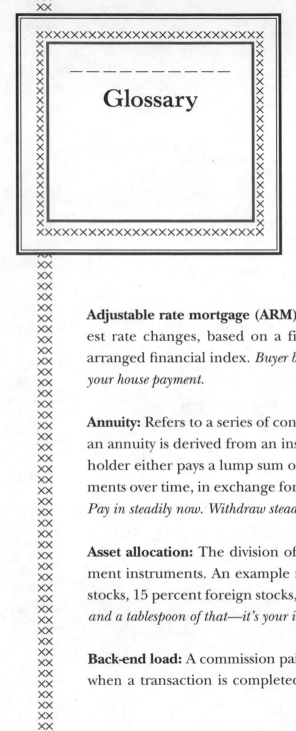

Glossary

Adjustable rate mortgage (ARM): A mortgage where the interest rate changes, based on a fixed time interval and a pre-arranged financial index. *Buyer beware! If interest rates rise, so will your house payment.*

Annuity: Refers to a series of continuous payments. Most often, an annuity is derived from an insurance plan where the policyholder either pays a lump sum of money or makes regular payments over time, in exchange for annuity payments later in life. *Pay in steadily now. Withdraw steadily later.*

Asset allocation: The division of money among various investment instruments. An example might be 35 percent domestic stocks, 15 percent foreign stocks, 50 percent bonds. *A cup of this and a tablespoon of that—it's your investment recipe.*

Back-end load: A commission paid by the investor, payable only when a transaction is completed. For example, in a back-end load mutual fund, the commission is paid when the shares are sold, as opposed to at the beginning of the transaction, when the shares are bought. The back-end load has the advantage that the investor can keep his or her money longer. *Like dining in a fancy restaurant, the bill doesn't come until you're ready to leave.*

Beneficiary: Any person or organization that receives financial benefits from an insurance policy, will, or trust fund. *Those who stand to benefit. Your husband or wife might be the beneficiary of your life insurance; your grandchildren might be among the beneficiaries in your will.*

Biweekly mortgage: A mortgage where the borrower makes a mortgage payment every two weeks, as opposed to once a month. On an annual basis, this results in an extra month's payment, thereby paying off the loan more quickly. *If you work a little harder in the beginning, the task becomes lighter in the end.*

Bond: A loan made to a corporation, government, or government agency that carries with it a specific interest rate and duration. The bearer (owner of the bond) is entitled to interest payments calculated at a specified rate (the coupon rate) and, when the specified time period is up, to the face value of the bond. Bonds are rated for safety (that is, the element of risk) by various rating agencies such as Standard and Poor's. "Triple A" is the best rating (lowest risk), and "C" is the lowest rating (highest risk). *They use the money to build a hospital and agree to pay you back at a certain time and with a certain amount of interest. How responsibly the county has behaved with borrowed money in the past, and how necessary the bigwigs believe the hospital is, determines the safety rating given to those bonds. Debt is not necessarily a bad thing so long as* the borrower uses the funds wisely, pays back promptly, and doesn't go to the well too often.

Broker: Any person or agency that arranges the buying and/or selling of securities for another person or agency. Brokers often are licensed and monitored by government agencies. *A wise broker is worth listening to but is no substitute for doing your own homework.*

Capital gains tax: A tax, currently up to 28 percent, on a gain realized when investments are sold. *It's the high-class worry that comes with making money.*

Capital gain or loss: The amount resulting when the original cost of a capital item is deducted from the selling price. If a gain results, the amount is subject to capital gains tax (see above). *Consider it your profit or loss.*

Certificate of deposit (CD): An investment with a financial institution. A fixed amount of money is deposited, for a specified period of time, at a predetermined interest rate, which generally does not change over the term of the instrument. *It's money in the bank, like a savings account, only you've agreed how long you'll leave it and the bank has agreed not to change the interest rate.*

Common stock: Stock that represents pro rata ownership in the company, and the stockholder, as a company owner, shares in the company's gains and losses. Common stock enables the owner of such stock (the shareholder) to vote on company actions. Should the company dissolve, the shareholders have the last claim on assets. *"It pays to know the company you keep."*

Compound interest: Interest calculated on both the principal amount as well as earned interest. As a result, capital increases much more quickly than if only simple interest were being calculated and paid. *Like a fast-growing plant in your garden, one little shoot makes two shoots, and the two shoots make four, the four make eight, and on and on and on.*

Convertible bond: A corporate bond that offers the bearer the option to acquire a predetermined amount of stock in the company instead of money when the bond is cashed in. The coupon rate on this kind of bond is generally lower than that of a regular corporate bond due to the value of the option. *You lose a little by taking a lower interest rate, but you could make it back in spades if the stock price rises.*

Corporate bond: (see *bond*) A certificate of corporate debt on which an investor gets paid interest. The instruments often represent a steady, high-yield investment. One drawback is that the income derived from these bonds is fully taxable (as opposed to the interest income from municipal or government bonds). *One way corporations borrow money.*

Diversification: The process of building a diverse investment portfolio, which includes different types of securities with different degrees of risk and maturity. *Computers are very popular today and so are big companies. But what about tomorrow? Since you can't predict the future, spread your money around in different industries, different size companies, different kinds of investments.*

Dividend: Company earnings that are distributed to stockholders paid out in a pro rata fashion. The amount of the dividend is decided by the company's board of directors and is dependent on the financial needs and plans of the company. In a quarter preceding large-scale development or expansion, for example, little or no dividends will be paid out. *A key way for a company's investors to share the wealth.*

Equity: The amount of ownership in a company. On a balance sheet, equity is defined as the difference between the assets and the liabilities. *Like a car or a home, you really own only the part that's paid for.*

Estate: Once a person dies, anything owned in that person's name, including property and proceeds from insurance policies, constitutes his or her estate. This also includes a share in any jointly owned assets. *All the things you leave behind.*

Executor: A person who manages an estate. The executor is named in the will and is responsible for probating the will (that is, supervising or performing legal procedures that prove to a court that someone has died). The executor supervises the distribution of the assets as directed in the will, often together with an estate lawyer. *Key person responsible for carrying out the wishes of the deceased. It might be a family member such as a brother or sister, or it might be a professional such as attorney or bank officer.*

Fixed assets: Assets that the owner is not planning or is unable to convert to cash in the short term. *For instance, stocks, real estate, and long-term CDs.*

Fixed-rate mortgage: A mortgage in which the amount of payments, including interest, are set at the time of the closing. The borrower knows exactly how much he or she will be paying for the entire term of the loan. *A deal you know will not change. The people loaning you the money agree not to change the amount you have to pay back or the interest rate.*

401(k) plan: A retirement plan that allows the employee to place a portion of his or her salary into a tax-sheltered account. Tax is deferred on these earnings until retirement, when the money is withdrawn. Many employers will match an employee's 401(k) contribution. *There's no such thing as a free lunch, but there is a subsidized lunch.*

Front-end load: A commission paid by the investor, payable when the transaction is initiated. For example, in a front-end load mutual fund, the commission is paid when the shares are bought, as opposed to when they are sold. (See also *Back-end load.*) *Like eating in a fast-food restaurant, you pay before you enjoy your meal.*

Growth assets: Assets in which the main objective is long-term growth rather than the generation of immediate income. For example, investing in stocks would be considered a growth asset because over time (say, 10 years) the returns have been historically higher than bank deposits; while a CD providing 8 percent for two years will provide an immediate return. *Mighty oaks from tiny acorns grow—but it takes time!*

Individual retirement account (IRA): A tax-deferred retirement account into which an individual may deposit up to a maximum of $2,000, provided that he or she is not contributing to any other retirement plan, such as a 401(k). The earnings are taxed only when they are withdrawn. Usually there is a penalty for withdrawing money from this account before a specified age (under current law, the age is 59 1/2). *Every year when you deposit* *your money, you can deduct that money from the total amount you pay taxes on. But you can't withdraw the money until your retirement age (when you will pay taxes on it), or else you pay a penalty.*

Inflation: A rise in the cost of goods and services. Inflation is measured by the Consumer Price Index, which compares current prices to an earlier benchmark year (currently 1967). The percentage increase in prices from the earlier year to the current year is the inflation rate. *Most of us can remember when gas was 12 cents per gallon.*

Intestate: The state of dying without a will. In such a case, the law of the state in which the deceased lived determines how and to whom the deceased's assets are distributed, and also if there are children under the age of 18, who shall be their guardian. *A host of problems can be avoided by making sure you have a will.*

Investment portfolio: The total holdings of an individual investor or institution. *The full list of what you have.*

Junk bond: A bond with a low rating (generally BB+ and below; see *Bonds*). They are issued by relatively weak or troubled companies that have a chance of recovery, thereby offering the investor the possibility of a high rate of return. *High risk in exchange for a potentially high payoff.*

Keogh plan: A retirement plan that allows self-employed people to make an annual tax-deductible contribution of up to 25 percent of his or her salary (up to $30,000). Tax is deferred on this money (and any interest it earns) until the sum is withdrawn upon retirement. *Self-employed person's version of a 401(k).*

Liabilities: An obligation (generally money) owed to another person or institution. *What you owe.*

Liquidity: A measure of how quickly investments may be converted into cash. Money kept in a checking account is highly liquid; equity in a house is less so. *Could you get your money if you needed it?*

Money market fund: A type of mutual fund that invests in short-term, relatively safe debt, such as government debt and that of highly rated corporations. *A low-risk investment giving you easy access to your money.*

Municipal bond: A bond issued by state or local governments, or agencies run by these governments (such as a state housing agency). These bonds usually have lower interest rates, but they are attractive because the interest earned on them generally is exempt from some or all taxes. *A good way to keep your interest tax-free, especially if you are in a high tax bracket.*

Mutual fund: A fund, sponsored by a company that sells shares in order to invest a large amount of money in various securities. The investors in the mutual fund then receive a proportional share of the increased or decreased value that the fund has realized on the various securities. The advantage of this type of fund is that it allows a person to invest in a diversified portfolio of stocks and bonds without the burden of having to learn about different investments. *You must trust the company sponsoring the fund to be doing their homework.*

Net worth: The difference between the value of assets over the value of liabilities. *You should evaluate your own net worth at least once a year.*

No-load: Means that no commission is charged. Generally used together with mutual funds, where the mutual fund charges neither on purchase nor sale of shares, although it may charge investment management fees. *Be sure to read the fine print.*

Pension: A retirement plan in which the retiree receives regular payments (an annuity) upon retirement, for the duration of the plan. Details of various retirement plans vary widely. *A good source but not to be relied on as the only source for retirement income.*

Preferred stock: Stock that, although it often carries no voting privileges, has claims to dividends and assets that take precedence over the claims of common stockholders. Preferred stock usually pays fixed dividends, and therefore the shareholder is not subject to the shifting fortunes of the company as common stockholders are. *Still, the value of the stock will still rise and fall.*

Rebalancing: The transfer of assets between accounts in a portfolio to maintain the original allocation percentages. This ensures a consistently well-balanced (or diversified) portfolio and may provide the investor with the opportunity to buy low and sell high. *Making sure you don't have everyone sitting in the same end of the canoe.*

Return on equity (ROE): The rate that is calculated by taking net income after taxes and dividing by the value of stock (the equity). The ROE gives an investor an idea of the efficiency of the company, since the higher the ROE, the more efficient the company's use of equity is. *Like checking the gas mileage your car gets. If the engine isn't running efficiently, you might need a tune-up.*

Return on investment (ROI): The rate that is calculated by taking net profit after taxes divided by total assets (including stocks and bonds). This number generally is used to evaluate a specific investment, such as a new piece of equipment or a new plant for a large corporation, as opposed to ROE (above), which evaluates the efficiency of a company. *A new freezer might pay for itself by allowing you to take advantage of big sales.*

Revenue bond: Bonds issued by government agencies in order to raise the funds to build facilities. These bonds may be risky because debt obligations often are derived only from the expected revenue from these projects. This means that if the projects turn out to be less profitable than expected, the investor may suffer a loss. *If you invest in a bridge no one drives over, it doesn't matter how high the toll is.*

Reverse mortgage: A mortgage where the homeowner is in effect allowing the bank to purchase his or her home. The bank (or other lending institution) pays money to the homeowner for the duration of his or her life. This is the opposite direction of the usual flow of money in a mortgage. The homeowner gets a fixed annuity; the bank gets the house on the homeowner's death. *A way for retirees to stay in their homes and receive money for living expenses, upkeep, and taxes.*

Salary Reduction Simplified Employee Pension Plan (SARSEPS): A tax-sheltered retirement plan in which the employee voluntarily puts part of his or her salary into a pension plan that can be invested. The interest earned on the investment, as well as the principal, is not taxed until withdrawn at retirement age (currently 59 1/2) Generally, the employee receives less salary, thus having less currently taxable income. This plan is similar to a 401(k) but is available only to companies with 25 employees or less. *A simple pension plan for small companies.*

Securities: Name for any type of investment, such as stocks and bonds. *Don't be fooled by the word. Securities are not necessarily secure.*

Simple interest: Interest is earned only on the principal investment, not on any accumulated interest payments. *Interest is always good, but compound interest is the best.*

Simplified Employee Pension Plan (SEP): A retirement plan designed for the self-employed and owners of small businesses. The SEP is simpler and more flexible than the Keogh plan. The policyholder contributes a fixed percentage of his or her net income, up to $30,000, which is tax-deductible, and the earnings are tax-deferred until the are withdrawn at retirement. *Self-employed people must take the initiative. No "company" is there to do it for you.*

Term life insurance: Insurance that protects the holder only for a specified period of time, called a "term." Term insurance is often the least expensive type of coverage, but it offers no payout if the holder survives through a term, as a whole life policy would. *Not much of an investment since the investor can never benefit.*

Trustee: A person who manages a trust. The name(s) and duties of trustees are usually outlined in the trust instrument itself. Trusts often are set up in wills to insure controlled use of assets for the benefit of beneficiaries. *If you were starting a trust for a young grandchild with the idea that he or she wouldn't receive the money until* *many years later, you would name a responsible person, possibly an of-ficer at the bank where you set up the trust, to oversee the money and carry out your wishes. A serious responsibility.*

Universal life insurance: The most flexible type of life insur-ance, universal life allows the policyholder to apply part of the savings to the cost of the insurance. The amount of the death benefit may be increased or decreased as long as the policy is in force. *A good way to keep your money working for you.*

U.S. Treasury bill: A government bond sold in minimum amounts of $10,000, with varying short-term maturity periods, no longer than 12 months. The interest rate is determined by the federal government and is used as a benchmark for a number of other securities and financial instruments (such as an ad-justable rate mortgage, for example). *Like the old savings bonds, but they mature very quickly.*

U.S. Treasury bond: Government bonds with maturity periods of 10 to 30 years, available in minimum amounts of $1,000. The interest rate is determined by the federal government. *Very high security.*

U.S. Treasury note: A government bond with a one- to 10-year maturity.

Vested pension: A pension in which the employee has an ab-solute right to the amount of the pension, regardless whether he or she changes jobs before retirement or not. *After a number of years of service, you become entitled to full benefits and you keep those benefits whether you stay, leave, or retire.*

Whole life insurance: The most traditional life insurance policy. The premiums are generally higher than that of term insurance policies and remain at the same amount for the length of the policy. At some point in the policy, the policyholder no longer has to make premium payments, but the policy remains in effect. The benefit is paid whenever the policyholder dies. Often the policyholder also can elect to receive an annuity or lump-sum payment after a certain age. *Life insurance plus an investment plan.*

Yield: The earnings derived from a security. The yield calculation differs from ROI because it should include any premium or discount paid for the investment vehicle. *Measuring how valuable the investment will be to you.*

Zero-coupon bond: A bond that is purchased for an amount that is far lower than its face value. Instead of collecting interest during the life of the bond, the investor cashes in the bond upon maturity for its full face value. *When you buy one of these bonds, you hold it until the date the government has agreed to pay you back, and then you get paid back with interest.*

INDEX

_ _ _ _ _ _ _ _ _ _ _ _ _ _

Entries in *italics* refer to tables and illustrations.

Accountant, *47*
Adjustable-rate mortgage (ARM), 129,
    234
  pros and cons, *130*
Adjusted basis, 134
A. G. Edwards, 105–6
A. M. Best ratings, *152*, 153
American Association of Retired Persons
    (AARP), 173
Amish Friendship Bread, 191–92
Amtrak Railways, 172
Annual Payment Factor table, *207*
Annuity
  defined, 85–86, 234; fees and penalities,
  86; vs. lump sum, 160, 161; post-
  retirement, *155*, 171, and preparing for
  retirement, 159
Annuity Factor table, *207*
Appraisal forms, *47*
Appraised value, 131
Asset allocation
  defined, 96, 234; how to figure,
  100–102; pies, *102;* post-retirement,
  155, 156–58; as recipe for success,
  96–98; and return, *101;* when to
  recalculate, 99–100; worksheets, 208–10
Assets
  adding up, 45; creating list, 47–50,
  143–44, 215–17; defined, 48; difficult-
  to-liquidate, 49; and estate planning,

139–40; evaluating, 48–49; hidden,
  58–61; liquid, 49–50; Social Security as,
  51–58
Atomos Energy, 106
Aunt Ruby's Salad, 175–76
Automatic deductions, 73
Avis Car Rental, 172

Back-end load, 113, 234–35
Balloon mortgage, 129
Bank accounts, avoiding fraud, 170
*Beardstown Ladies' Common-Sense Investment
    Guide, The,* 2–3, 30, 105, 171, 178–79
Beardstown Ladies' Investment Club
  appeal of, 204; average return of, 3;
  compound interest and, 30; education
  sessions, 137; our best budget tips,
  71–72; and pay yourself first principle,
  7–8; planning theme, 46; projects and
  pastimes, 174–204; record year, 3;
  sudden fame of, 1–6; video, 233
Beneficiaries, 141, 235
Better Investing magazine, 175
Bills
  and budgeting, 68–69; and net worth,
  50; and paying yourself first, 74
Biweekly mortgage, 129–30, 235
Blue-chip stocks, 93
Bonds, 47
  and asset allocation, 100–101, 104;

Bonds (cont.)
  defined, 107, 235–36; pros and cons, 107–8; ratings, 235–36; vs. stocks, 106; types of, 107–12
Book value, 131
Brewer, Ann, 6, 59, 74, 77, 115, 154–55, 165, *175*
  projects and pastimes, 175–76
Broker, 236
Budget
  defined, 45; how to create, 67; vs. managing money, 64; and needs vs. wants, 70–71; our best tips on, 71–72; and preparing for retirement, 159; ten steps to, 68–69; worksheets, 212–14
Business, starting, 99
Business segments, 95
"Buy low, sell high" rule, 97

Cap, 129
Capital gain or loss, 236
Capital gains tax, 236
Car
  expenses, 65, 71, 72; insurance, 71; loans, 50
Career
  field, 59; switching, 15
Cash assets worksheet, 209
Cash equivalent, 96
Cash expenses, tracking, 67–68
Cash-value life insurance, 149–51, *151*
  and preparing for retirement, 159–60
Catalogs, 73
CBS This Morning (TV show), 3
Certificates of deposit (CDs)
  defined, 96, 236; vs. diversified investments, 91, 104; post-retirement, *155;* pros and cons, 112; risk of, 93; and tax penalties, 49
Charities, 170
Checking accounts, 47, 138
  savings notation, 73
Children
  and asset allocation, 99; as hidden asset, 60; and life insurance, 146; and will, 141–42
Choice Hotel International, 172
Closing costs, 126
Coins, 49
Collectibles
  Ann Corley's Depression era glassware, 177–78; Betty's antique glass and crystal, 199; Carnell's ceramic pigs, 190; pros and cons of, 104, 118–19
College
  and asset allocation, 99; financial

  planning for, 18; as investment, 59–60; saving for, 14, 59
Colorado state parks, 173
Combination Keogh, 87
Commodities, 93
Common stock, 236
Compound interest
  calculating, 28–29; and credit cards, 41–42; defined, 26–29, 237, 244; how to take advantage of, 29–33, 44; and inflation, 25; and interest rates, *40;* and mortgage, 128; penny example of, 34–35, *35–36*
Continental Airlines, 172
Continuing care retirement communities, 168–69
Convertible bond, 237
Corley, Ann, 5, 46, 96–97, 104, 138–39, *177*
  projects and pastimes, 176–78
Corley, Larry, 177
Corporate bonds
  defined, 110, 237; mutual funds for, 114; and post-retirement, *155;* pros and cons of, 110; risk of, 93; vs. stocks, 106
Coupons, 73
Credit cards
  avoiding fraud, 170; and compound interest, 41–42; diet, 72; and net worth, 50

Days Inn, 172
Day-to-day spending and savings plan, 64
Debt repayment, 18
Deferred fixed-rate annuity, 85, 86
Deferred variable annuity, 85, 86
Dickinson, Peter, 164
Disability insurance, 18
  Social Security as, 52
Diversification, 90–98
  and asset allocation, 100–102; defined, 91, 237; *See also* Asset allocation
Dividends
  defined, 91, 105, 237–38; shares as, 105–6
Divorce
  and asset allocation, 99; and Social Security, 58
Doctor visits, 65
Dollar cost averaging, 97, *98*
Domestic stocks, 96
Donahue (TV show), 1–2, 6, 187, 196
"Double Dutch Chocolate Cream Pie" investment set, 102
"Down averaging," 97
Dried Flower Wreath instructions, 186

Econo-Lodge, 172
Education, as asset, 58–60
Edwards, Doris, 64–65, 91, 159, *179*
  projects and pastimes, 178–81
Einstein, Albert, 28, 44
Elder Cottage Housing Opportunity
  (ECHO), 169
Ellis, Lillian, 64, 137, 141, 176, 177, 200
Employer, and retirement, 159
Entertainment expenses, 65, 67, 71–72
Equity
  in house, 131–32; stock, 238
Estate
  defined, 238; taxes, 140
Estate planning
  defined, 138–40; and life insurance,
  146–47; reason for, 136–37; worksheet,
  140, 215–17
Executor, 141, 142, 238
Expenses
  categories, 65, 68; worksheets, 212,
  213–14; *See also* Budget; Spending

Family
  death in, and asset allocation, 99; Doris
  on importance of, 180–81; as hidden
  asset, 60
Farming, 53, 93–94, 99, 116, 120, 189,
  194–95
  how finances are like, 64–65
Financial advisor, 49
  and fraud, 169, 170
"Financial Mastery" seminar, 4–5
Financial planning, 64
  books on, 226–27; defined, 10–11; and
  figuring needs after retirement, 158;
  how to begin, 12–18; magazines on,
  228–29; organizations for, 222–23; and
  selling house, 133
Fixed assets, 238
Fixed expenses
  and budgeting, 68; cutting, 71;
  worksheets, 212, 213–14
Fixed-income assets, 95, 96
  worksheet, 209
Fixed-rate mortgage, 129, 238–39
  pros and cons, *130*
Food spending, 65
  creating targets, 66; shopping tips, 73
Foreign bond mutual funds, 114
Foreign stocks, 95, 96
401(k)s, 77
  borrowing from balance, 82; defined,
  80–83, 239; vs. IRA, 85; lump-sum vs.
  annuity, 160–61; mobility of, 82–83;
  pros and cons of, 79, *79*

403(b)s, 80
Franklin, Benjamin, 26, 44
Fraud, 169–71
Frisch's Restaurants, 172
Front-end load, 113, 239
"Full retirement age," 56–57, *57*
Funeral "prepayment," 170–71
Futures, 93

Gaushell, Dennis, 181
Gaushell, Sharon, 181
Gaushell, Sylvia, 69, 122, 125, *182*
  projects and pastimes, 181–83
Generic brands, 71
Geographic diversification, 95
Gifts
  and estate taxes, 140; offering service
  as, 72; and preparing for retirement,
  159–60
Goals
  defining, 13–14; life, 17–18; planning to
  pay for, 18; and retirement, 158
Gold, 104, 117–18
  mutual funds, 114
Government bonds, 91
  pros and cons of, 108–9; time frame of,
  95
Graduated payment mortgage, 129
Gross, Shirley, 1, 6, 14, 30, 46, 53, 77, 105,
  115, 137, 138, 176–77, *183*, 204
  projects and pastimes, 183–84
Growing equity mortgage, 129
Growth assets or stocks, 95, 239
  and diversifying, 96; post-retirement,
  155; risk of, 93
Guardian, 141, 142

Health insurance, 18
  amount needed, 148; premiums, 65;
  and preparing for retirement, 159
Health issues
  books on, 227; magazines on, 230;
  organizations for, 223–24
Heart of Illinois Council, 176
High-risk investments, 93, *94*
Holographic will, 142
Home health care, 158, 165–66
Home insurance, 71
Home items expenses, 65
"Homemade Apple Pie" investment set,
  102
Horse breeding, 185
Houchins, Jerry, 184–85
Houchins, Margaret, 2, 4, 5, 34, 51, 86,
  106, 147–48, *185*
  projects and pastimes, 184–86

House brands, 71
"Household Budget" books, 69
House (home), 120–35
  appreciation, 121–22; and asset allocation, 99; costs, 18; and equity, 131–32; how to buy, 122–26; and mortgage, 126–31; and net worth, 48–49; selling, 132–33, 159; taxes and, 49, 133–35; values of, 131
House improvements
  avoiding fraud, 171; and taxes, 134; value of, 125–26, 127, 133
Housing, and retirement, 165–69
Howard Johnson hotels, 173
Huston, Dale, 122, 187
Huston, Norman, 122, 187
Huston, Ruth, 2, 63, 91, 122, 125, 165–66, 187
  projects and pastimes, 187–88

Illustration (life insurance), 150–51
Immediate annuity, 85
Individual retirement accounts (IRAs), 16, 77, 91
  defined, 83–85, 239–40; vs. 401(k), 85; and lump-sum payouts, 160; and preparing for retirement, 159; pros and cons of, 78–79, 78, 83–85; records, 47; selling, 159
Inflation
  defined, 240; and bonds, 108; and retirement saving, 23–25, 24; vs. stocks, 106
Inheritance (state) taxes, 140
Insurance
  cutting costs of, 71; Planner worksheet, 218; records, 47; See also Health insurance; Life insurance
Interest rates (rate of return)
  calculating compound, 28; and credit cards, 41–42; and how long retirement money will last, 157; and mortgage payments, 126–28; and refinancing mortgage, 71; and savings, 38–41, 40
Internal Revenue Service, 53, 88, 114, 134
  publications list, 230–33
Intestate, 140–41, 142, 240
Inventory, 59
Investment clubs, 171
Investment portfolio
  defined, 64, 240; post-retirement, 155
Investments
  assessing value of, 49; and asset allocation, 96–102; and asset allocation, after retirement, 155; and avoiding fraud, 169–71; balancing, 93–98;

diversifying, 90–92, 95; home ownership as, 121–35; learning about, 91; and lump sum payout, 160–61; "pies," 102; and preparing for retirement, 159; post-retirement, 154, 155–58, 171; and retirement funds, 77–78; return, and asset allocation, 100–102, 101; and return vs. risk, 92–95, 94; taxable vs. tax-deferred, 78–79, 78; telling heirs about, 139; types, 104–119; whole life insurance as, 149–50
Invoices, 47

Jobs, changing, 99
Junk bonds
  defined, 240; risk of, 93, 111–12

Keoghs, 47, 77
  advantages of, 78; defined, 240; how to set up, 87–88; lump-sum vs. annuity, 160–61; types, 87
Korsmeyer, Carnell, 4, 5, 6, 17, 23, 35, 93–94, 99, 171, 189
  projects and pastimes, 188–90
Kramer, Helen, 62–63, 120, 155, 191
  projects and pastimes, 191–92

Lawyer, 49, 141–42
Layoffs, 15
Legal resources, 226
Leisure time, 72
"Lemon Meringue Pie" investment set, 102
Liabilities
  defined, 45, 241; creating list, 50–51; worksheets, 208, 211
Life expectancy
  and annuity, 160; chart, 19–23, 21; and post-retirement investments, 156
Life insurance, 18, 71, 122
  avoiding fraud, 171; chart comparing, 151; company ratings, 151–53, 152; defined, 146–49; and estate planning, 139; how much you need, 147–48; and preparing for retirement, 159–60; reason for, 136, 137; types, 149–53; when you need, 146–47
Limited partnerships, 49, 171
Limited-risk investments, 93, 94
Lindahl, Hazel, 1, 46, 60–61, 70, 72, 121, 165, 167, 170, 193
  projects and pastimes, 193–94
Liquid assets, 49
Living will, 145
Loans, paying off, 72

Long-term bonds, 96
Low-risk investments, 93, *94*
Lump sum payout, 160–69

McCombs, Bill, 67, 80, 194
McCombs, Carol, 2, 6, 19, 59–60, 67, 74,
    80, 84, 107, *195,* 196
  projects and pastimes, 194–95
McCombs, Cindy, 194
McCombs, Jennifer, 194
McCombs, Marty, 194
McDonald's stock, 106
Major purchases, planning for, 69
Margaret, Aunt, 20, 199
Marriage, 99
MCI, 112
Medicaid
  and nursing home, 167; requirements,
  158
Medical expenses, 65, 66
Medicare, 52
  and nursing home, 167; and preparing
  for retirement, 158, 159; tax, 52–53;
  when to apply for, 160
Medigap policies, 158
Merck stock, 96–97
Michel, Robert, 181
Ministers, 53
"Mobile" pensions, 77
Moderate-risk investments, 93, *94*
Money
  figuring how long it will last after
  retirement, 156–58, *157;* hiding, 138
Money market funds, 121, 47
  defined, 112–13, 241; post-retirement,
  155; risk of, 93
Money-purchase Keogh, 87
Monthly income, 66, 68
Monthly spending, 66
Moody's, 110, *152,* 153
Mortgage, 65, 126–31
  and net worth, 50; refinancing, 71;
  types defined, 129–30
Municipal bonds
  defined, 109, 241; mutual funds, 114;
  pros and cons, 109–10
Municipal bonds, 93
Mutual funds
  and compound interest, 30, *30–32,*
  38–39; defined, 112–14, 241; and
  diversification, 95; fees or load, 113–14;
  post-retirement, 171; pros and cons,
  104, 114–15

National Association of Investors
  Corporation, 106, 171

National Association of Realtors, 125
National Fraud Information Center,
  169–70
National Insurance Consumer
  Organization, 151
"Necessary" list, 18
Net worth
  defined, 241; and hidden assets, 58;
  figuring, 44–51; and preparing for
  retirement, 158; reason to know yours,
  46
Net worth statement
  defined, 45; forms, 47; how to make,
  47–51; and managing money, 64;
  updating, 50; where to keep, 47;
  worksheets, 51, 208–11
New York Times, 2
No-load, 113–14, 242
Nonfixed (variable) expenses, 65, 68
  worksheets, 212, 214
Nonviable rating, 151, *152*
Nursing home care, 158, 166–68

Options, 93

Part-time work, 159
Payroll deductions, for savings, 74
Pay yourself first principle
  and budgeting, 69; and compound
  interest, 34; defined, 7–8; developing
  habit of, 62–65; how we do it, 73–74
Penalty on early withdrawal, 82, 85
Penny example, 34, *35, 37*
Pension plans, 47
  defined, 242; how to take money out of,
  160–61; and preparing for retirement,
  159; problems with, 77
Personal assets worksheet, 210
Points, 126
Post-retirement investments, 154–73
  and asset allocation, *155*
Post retirement living, 154–55
  and deciding where to live, 161–64
Power of attorney, 145
Precious metals, 114
Preferred stock, 242
Prescriptions, 65
"Prizes," 170
Profit-sharing Keogh, 87
Profit-sharing plans, 160–61
Property taxes, 65

Ramey, Clara and Donald, 26
Ramey family, 26–27, 38
Real estate, 47, 59
  assets worksheet, 209; and estate

Real Estate *(cont.)*
  planning, 139; as investment type, 104;
  location, 123; pros and cons of, 115–17;
  risk, 93
Rebalancing, 97–98, 242
  vs. recalculating, 99–100
Recalculating, 99–100
Recipes
  Amish Friendship Bread, 191–92; Aunt
  Ruby's Salad, 176
Records
  keeping good, 142–43; and preparing
  for retirement, 159
Rent, 65
Repairs vs. purchases, 72
Resources, 222–33
Restricted stock, 49
Retirement
  age at, and Social Security, 56–58, *58;*
  avoiding fraud during, 169–71; creating
  financial plan for, 18; deciding where
  to live, 161–64; defined, 14–16;
  discounts and deals during, 172–73;
  figuring out how much money you
  need for, 19–25; figuring out if you're
  ready for, 158–60; how much you need
  to save annually for, *22;* housing,
  165–69; importance of saving for, 7–8;
  inflation and, 23–25, *24;* investments
  after, 156–58, *155;* lifestyles books, 228;
  lifestyles organizations, 224–26; planner
  worksheet, 206–7; projects and
  pastimes, 174–204; readiness reminder
  checklist, 158–59; and reverse
  mortgage, 130–31; saving for, 14; and
  selling house, 134–35; and Social
  Security, 51, 52–58; videos on, 233;
  what to do if you don't think your
  money will last, 157; when to start
  thinking about, 15–16
Retirement accounts
  benefits, and estate planning, 139; how
  to take money out of, 160–62; setting
  up, 76–89; and tax penalties, 49;
  worksheets, 210
Retirement communities, 166
Retirement Letter, 164
Return
  and asset allocation, 100–102, *101;* on
  bonds, 109; defined, 92–95
Return on equity (ROE), 242
Return on investment (ROI), 243
Revenue bonds, 109, 243
Reverse mortgage, 129, 130–31,
  243
Reward, 92–95

Rieken, Homer, 30
Risk
  defined, 92–93; and diversification, 92;
  and investing lump-sum payout, 161; of
  municipal bonds, 109; vs. reward, 92–95
"Risk-reward" ratio, 93–94, *94*
  of stocks, 106
Robbins, Tony, 4–5
RPM stock, 91

Safe deposit box, 138
Salary Reduction Simplified Employee
    Pension Plan (SARSEP), 88, 243–44
Sales, 72
Saving
  annual, for retirement, *22;* and
  compound interest, 27–28, 30–35,
  35–36; economizing to find money for,
  37; figuring out how much is required,
  19–25; how to develop habit, 62–65;
  and inflation, 23–25, *24;* and interest
  rates, 38–41; and monthly budget,
  68–69, 73; start with small amounts, 74;
  teaching children about, 34–35; time to
  start, 8, 23, 35–37; tips on, 71–73
Savings accounts
  for college education, 59; importance
  of having, 69; letting people know
  about, 138; and net worth statement,
  47; and risk vs. reward, 93
Savings Growth Factor table, *207*
Scandinavian Airlines, 173
Schedule SE, 53
Scheer, Elsie, 2, 6, 116, 137, 147, 171, 194,
    196
  projects and pastimes, 196–97
Securities, 244
Self-employment
  and Medicare tax, 53; and Social
  Security taxes, 53; and tax-deferred
  retirement plans, 86–88, 240, 244
Shopping tips, 72, 73
Short-term bonds, 96
Simple interest, 28–29, 244
Simplified Employee Pension plans
    (SEPs), 77, 88, 244
Single-premium annuity, 85–86
Sinnock, Betty, 3, 4, 5, 14, 79, 81, *198*
  projects and pastimes, 197–99
Sinnock, Bob, 198–99
Smith, Harry, 3
Social Security, 22, 51–58
  applying for, 160; as asset, 51; benefits
  schedule by age, *57;* defined, 51–52;
  figuring your benefit, 54–55; monthly
  benefit chart, *56;* payroll deduction,

52–53; post-retirement, 155; and preparing for retirement, 159, 160; when you can collect, 56–58; who qualifies for, 53–54
Social Security Administration, how to contact, 54–55
Speculative stocks, 93
Spending
  and budget, 68–69; cutting down, 64, 67–68, 70–73; sorting out, 65–67; *See also* Budget; Expenses
Spouse
  and life insurance, 147; nonworking, and Social Security, 54
Stamps, 49
Standard & Poor's 500, 106
  investment ratings, 110; life insurance ratings, 152–53, *152*
Stock broker, 47
Stock(s)
  advantages of, 106–7; and asset allocation, 96–97, 100–101, 104; assets worksheet, 209; and compound interest, 33, 41; defined, 105–7; and diversification, 91, 95; and estate planning, 139; mutual funds, 93, 115; and net worth statement, 47; picking, 2–3; and rebalancing, 97–98; risk, 93; splits, 105–6; *see also* Investment portfolio
Student loans, 50, 60
Superior rating, 151, *152*

Tax-deferred retirement plans, 76–88
  annuities, 85–86; eligibility, 83–84; 401(k)s, 79–82; importance of, 77–78; IRAs, 83–85; Keogh plans, 87–88; for self-employed, 86–88; SEPs, 88; types, 78–79
Taxes
  and asset liquidation, 49; and cashing in IRAs, 159; and estate planning, 140; and lump-sum vs. annuity, 160–61; and selling house, 133–35; and where to live after retirement, 162; and whole life insurance, 149–50
Telephone
  and account information, 47; hotlines, 233; investment precautions, 169–70
Templeton World Fund, *30–32*
"10-Year Lease—Option to Buy" plan, 99–100
Term life insurance, 149, *151*, 244
Term of mortgage, 128
TGI Friday's, 173

Thomas, Maxine, 3, 4, 5, 20, 64, 148, 176, 177, *201*, 204
  projects and pastimes, 200–201
Thomas, Roy, 200
Tillitt-Pratt, Buffy, 2, 4, 5, 15–16, 59, 100, 115–16, 122–23, 126, 129, *203*
  projects and pastimes, 202–4
Tillitt-Pratt, T. J., 16, 202–4, *203*
Time frame, 95–96
Timing the market, 98
Transportation expenses, 72
Traveling, 180, 200
Trustee, 141, 142, 244–45
20/20 (TV show), 3, 6, 196

United Airlines, 173
U. S. savings bonds, 108
U. S. Treasury bill
  defined, 96, 108, 245; rates, and mortgages, 129; vs. stocks, 106; time frame, 95
U. S. Treasury bonds
  defined, 108, 245; mutual funds, 114; risk, 93
U. S. Treasury note, 245
Universal life insurance, 149, 150, *151*, 245
Utilities, 65
  bonds, 110

Variable expenses. *See* Nonfixed expenses
Variable life insurance, 150, *151*
Vested pensions, 49, 245
Videos, 72, 233
Volunteer work, 201

Wall Street Journal, 49, 106
Where to Retire magazine, 163–64
Whole life insurance, 149–50, *151*, 246
Widowhood
  and estate planning, 139; and life insurance, 147–48; and Social Security, 58
Wills
  how to prepare, 141–44; importance of, 136–37, 140–41; revising, 142; sample, 220–21
"Wish List," 17–18
Women, and retirement, 155
Worksheets, 206–18

"Yellow padding," 16–17
Yield, 246
  and whole life insurance, 150

Zero-coupon bonds, 93, 111, 246

The Beardstown Ladies are 15 women who are members of an investment club that was established more than 12 years ago. They all live in or near Beardstown, Illinois, and still meet on the first Thursday of every month.

Robin Dellabough is a senior editor at Seth Godin Productions. A former freelance writer, she has worked on more than a dozen books and is the author of *Students Shopping for a Better World* and *101 Ways to Get Straight A's*.

Seth Godin Productions creates books and CD ROMs in Irvington-on-Hudson, New York. To date, they have more than 75 titles in print, including works on business, celebrities, computers, and more.

THE BEARDSTOWN LADIES

Cookin' Up Profits on Wall Street

RETURNS **59.5%** RETURNS
in 1991

A Guide to Common Sense Investing

NOW MEET THE LADIES IN THEIR OWN VIDEO!

Shot on location in Beardstown, Illinois this one hour video gives you the flavor and spirit of the Ladies "up close and personal." The Beardstown Ladies' award-winning videotape, *Cookin' Up Profits on Wall Street*, tells you everything you need to know to create your own common-sense financial plan, organize and run your own investment club, and look for companies using the same fundamentals the Ladies use. It includes interviews with all of the members of the club as well as point by point explanations of key areas. Great for individual investors or investment clubs, old or new!

Mature Media
1994 ℠
NATIONAL AWARDS
WINNER

Gold Medal Winner
National Mature Marketing Award

Winner,
National Media Owl Award

"Of the financial videos . . . the most entertaining."—*MONEY* magazine

"A superb guide for potential investment club organizers . . . as well as individual investors."—*Booklist*

To order your own copy at $10.00 off the regular price of $29.95, call.

1-800-359-3276

MasterCard, Visa, or Discover accepted. Ask for offer #27. Or use the coupon below for check or money order.

- -

NAME _____

ADDRESS _____

CITY _____ STATE _____ ZIP _____

YES! Please rush me ____ VHS copies of *Cookin' Up Profits on Wall Street* at $19.95 plus $4.95 shipping and handling each. (Illinois residents please add sales tax at 6.25%)

I have enclosed my check or money order for _____.
Mail to: Central Picture Entertainment, Inc., Video Order Dept., P.O. Box 578–219, Chicago, IL 60657–8219.
Please allow 4–6 weeks for delivery.